Website & Marketing Mistakes Coaches Make:

12 Critical Mistakes That REPEL Your Ideal Clients ...And How To Avoid Them!

Brad Reed

www.CoachesMarketingToolbox.com

Copyright Notice

Disclaimers

The information, instructions, and advice contained in this publication are for educational purposes only. Brad Reed, and Transformation Bay LLC, and the content of this publication cannot be relied upon as treatment, cure, or for prevention of any business or life situation. It is recommended that you consult with a qualified practitioner before acting on or implementing any of the information or recommendations made in this publication. Any use of the information contained in this publication is at your own risk. Because there is always some risk associated with and involved in making life and business changes, Brad Reed, and Transformation Bay LLC are not responsible for any consequences or adverse effects of any kind resulting from the use or misuse of any information, instructions, suggestions, or advice described in this publication. The information is provided "as is" without any representations or warranties, expressed or implied. The reader and/or possessor of these materials assume all risk from non-use, misuse, or use of this information.

The information presented in this publication represents the views of the author at the time of publication. Because conditions change and new information is published or revealed frequently, the author reserves the right to update or alter his opinion based on the new information and conditions. While best efforts have been used in preparing the information in this publication, the author assumes no responsibility for errors, inaccuracies, or omissions. Any slights of people or organizations are unintentional.

Affiliate Link Disclaimer

Please assume that any links in this document are affiliate links. If you were to purchase through one of these links I may receive some compensation for that purchase.

Some of the links in this document may go directly to the products and/or services that I offer, or that are offered as part of my business under Transformation Bay LLC or other businesses with which I have association.

The included affiliate links are for products and services that I have used, or come recommended by sources I personally trust. While I cannot vouch for any product or service that I have not personally created or deliver, there are many excellent products and services of which I am aware and have confidence in and thus feel comfortable recommending.

In the event that you do not wish to purchase through these affiliate links, you may use other means to locate these products or services through your favorite search engine on the web. I appreciate your support through the use of these affiliate links, but it is not required.

A Special "Thank You"

I have to say a special "Thank you!" top Pattie Craumer for her feedback and editing help. Her input and sharp eye definitely helped make this book even better!

Other Books & DVDs By Brad Reed

These are available at the time of initial publication of this book. More may have been published since then. For an updated list please visit: http://CoachesMarketingToolbox.com/published

Books:

Fast Migraine Headache Relief With EFT Tapping

Available on Amazon.com - http://amzn.to/1jgbibf

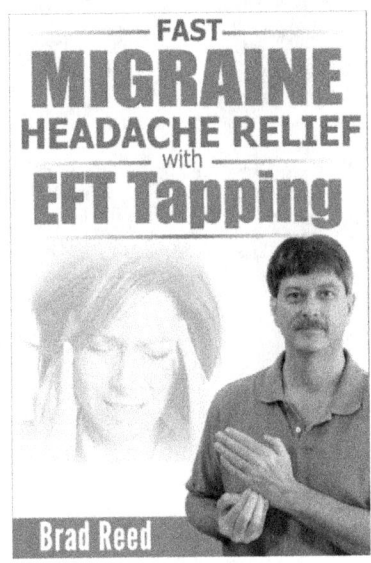

DVD's:

The Secret For Law Of Attraction – What the gurus aren't telling you

Available on Amazon.com - `http://amzn.to/1gHVBYs`

Contents

Other Books & DVDs By Brad Reed.......................v

Author Bio xi

Introduction..1

Chapter 1: Look Mommy, I made a website!............9

Chapter 2: My ideal clients abhor Social Media. Besides, I've got a blog!......................................19

Chapter 3: CoachFluffyBunny@AOL.com..............27

Chapter 4: I found it free on the internet so I can use it...right? 35

Chapter 5: I'm coaching them; they don't really care what I look like!..47

Chapter 6: I'll break the Internet if I do something wrong!...55

Chapter 7: Nobody would ever guess......................63

Chapter 8: I can't share that, it's confidential! 77

Chapter 9: I'm busy! Besides, it really doesn't matter because they'll just read about it anyway 87

Chapter 10: I don't want to annoy people. They'll call me when they are ready. 95

Chapter 11: If they are interested they will know what to do. There is no need to manipulate them105

Chapter 12: The Internet never goes down, besides my site is too small to hack! 113

Conclusion...129

Recommended Resources 143

Don't Get Left Behind!

Your Personal Invitation from Brad Reed

Because you bought my book, I'd like to invite you to visit my Coaches Marketing Toolbox blog and subscribe for updates and a Bonus Chapter! When you sign up, I will make sure you can get the latest insights into what's working in the world of effectively marketing your coaching business.

If you want to learn what is working when it comes to creating your attractive and effective coaching website, marketing your coaching business, and selling higher ticket coaching packages to your ideal clients, then here's what I'd like to invite you to do.

Go ahead and visit `http://www.CoachesMarketingToolbox.com/book` and sign up for a free account. It takes about 30 seconds and could very well revolutionize the results you get from your marketing and your coaching website.

By signing up you'll be able to get all the latest developments in refining your Ideal Client Avatar so you can speak directly to your ideal client every time, generating interesting and relevant content for your coaching blog that will magnetize your ideal clients to you, and creating an awesome website that you are proud to call your own and show your clients.

So as you are enjoying this book and want to take your coaching website and marketing practices to the next level, head on over to `http://www.CoachesMarketingToolbox.com/book` and get onboard for free. Do it now.

P.S. When you sign up now you will also get access to **Chapter 13:** *Google Is Going To LOVE My Brand New Website!* which is not include in this book. So sign up now and get this exclusive Bonus Chapter!

Author Bio

My name is Brad Reed and I have been coaching and advising people since the 1990's and have been studying and using modern online marketing techniques since 2008. This book contains just a small slice of what I've learned and know to be effective in these areas.

I am an Electrical Engineer by training, and spent a good portion of my career in sales, marketing and (international) technical customer support. I have been using, teaching, and coaching people using EFT (Emotional Freedom Technique) for about 15 years. My first book, Fast Migraine Headache Relief With EFT Tapping, is sold internationally.

My coaching skills, along with my marketing knowledge, are hard won through studying with and watching a variety of mentors and "gurus" in a variety of markets over the years. I have seen what they say works, and have experienced what actually works.

I know the details of marketing effectively on the internet. I've built websites from scratch, created products, wrote sales copy, created graphics, wrote shot and edited videos, and have even turned them into a DVD which is available on my website and Amazon.com. I have lived what I'm sharing with you here in this book.

Part of the reason that I wrote this book was my experience as an adjunct staff member for a year-long EFT Tapping and business development program. It was created and delivered by one of my good friends who is a celebrity in the EFT Tapping world. I have watched her grow her coaching business well into the 7-figure realm in the last few years. My job on the team was primarily helping the students with technology, including video production, website creation, autoresponders, and more. Many of the students were coaches themselves. Creating a thriving coaching practice was the primary focus of the business building material taught in the program.

I can honestly say that if I had not learned the material in the "coaching business" training section of her program I would not have been able to close the $6,000 coaching deal that I landed today for a seven session coaching package. Coaching can be a very lucrative business when you know how to speak your ideal customer's language in a way that shows you understand their problems, concerns and pains, and you have a way to help resolve the issues that are driving their need and desire for coaching.

I love teaching, problem solving, and helping people be even more successful than they already are in life. I teach what I know. I listen, analyze and discover when I'm problem solving. I light up and enjoy life even more when I get to help people be even more successful.

Bottom line: I help coaches build a thriving practice with the website and marketing knowledge I share with them so they can have even more success and create an even larger income.

For speaking or consulting inquiries, please contact me through the Coaches Marketing Toolbox Website at
`http://CoachesMarketingToolbox.com/contact`

I'd also like to invite you to visit the Coaches Marketing Toolbox blog and subscribe so you can receive updates and the latest insights into what's working in the world of effectively marketing your coaching business. Simply point your web browser to `http://www.CoachesMarketingToolbox.com/book` and sign up for free.

Introduction

Welcome!

Welcome to Website & Marketing Mistakes Coaches Make: 12 Critical Online Mistakes That REPEL Your Ideal Clients! I wrote this book because I have watched friends and colleagues who are coaches, and have seen what they go through. I see them struggle unnecessarily while creating their marketing message, their website, and getting enough new coaching clients to have a full and profitable coaching practice.

They have great coaching skills, tools, and techniques because of their in-depth coach training, but what they lack is modern marketing training and skills. One of my friends showed me the "marketing section" of her training manual. It had examples of marketing material and flyers from 1996, and she was taking her training in 2014! Needless to say, while some aspects of those approaches are evergreen others have gone the way of the dinosaur.

The vast majority of coaches rely on word-of-mouth and networking to fill their practices. Unfortunately, even if you are an outstanding coach with all kinds of training and skills, that doesn't automatically make you someone who is great at marketing your business or even know how to network effectively.

I have been coaching people in various capacities since the 1990's and have been studying and using modern online marketing techniques since 2008. This book contains a small slice of what I've learned and know to be effective in this area.

While this book talks about the 12 Critical Online Mistakes That REPEL Your Ideal Clients, you will also find included in each chapter not only why they are mistakes, but also how to fix them, how to prevent them from happening again, and my best advice for being successful in each of the 12 areas once you move away from making the mistake. Some of these mistakes simply aren't your fault either. I'm willing to wager that you have never even considered some of these before, let alone know how to quickly and easily eliminate these mistakes.

Special Disclaimers

It goes without saying that I am not a lawyer, and I don't even play one on TV. So when it comes to implementing what you learn in this book please be sure to seek professional counsel, especially in any areas where you have questions. Copyrights, client confidentiality, email marketing (CANSPAM rules) and the FTC's view on "marketing claims" at a minimum are areas where seeking counsel from a knowledgeable professional will help you stay out of trouble.

Key Points We'll Cover

You probably bought this book because you want to know how to effectively market your coaching business on the Internet and how to have a professional looking website that consistently brings in new coaching clients. You also don't want to make website and marketing mistakes that would repel your clients, because you recognize that marketing is the engine that brings coaching clients to you, and puts money in your pocket.

The first chapter addresses websites and the often overlooked key viewpoint that you must use when you build your website...and every other piece of marketing material that you ever create. The information on FRED is likely to change every marketing message you create...forever!

The second chapter ends the debate about blogs, and social media use in your coaching business. It also shows exactly where vanity belongs in your business, and there is a definite spot for it! There is one specific tip in this chapter could save you hours every week. Don't miss it!

In Chapter three we will address Email professionalism and the deadly mistake that can completely destroy your credibility in the eyes of your potential ideal client. Fortunately, the fix for this mistake is not only simple but when done right it can save you from having to remember yet another password.

The fourth chapter introduces "theft on the Internet" and what can happen if you do it, even inadvertently, and how to keep yourself from accidentally falling into the trap that is waiting for you there. This chapter should remove any question about the value of "playing by the rules" and the consequences if you don't! "Big Brother" is watching and you can stay off his RADAR by knowing how to use this information in your coaching business.

The value of putting a face on your business is covered in chapter five. Knowing when to change that face is just as important and is covered in this chapter as well.

Chapter six covers who is qualified, and how to stay out of trouble, when it comes to creating or modifying your website. Content may be king, but it's the manicured royal gardens that bring in the clients who want to smell the roses, and are willing to pay you for that privilege. So don't hire the court jester as the gardener!

The seventh chapter may scare you and immediately cause you to run to your computer to make some vital changes to your bank account. The solution for this mistake is easy, but the consequences of making it can be extremely costly.

Introduction

This is one of two chapters you do not want to skip if you value your sanity and security.

Client confidentiality is probably a natural part of your coaching practice. In chapter eight you will learn ways to get around that confidentiality and use your clients' personal results to promote your business...and keep everyone happy while doing it!

Chapter nine shows you how to enlist that "blunt" friend of yours – you know the one, they always "say it like it is" without any sugar coating – and have them help save your business. There are so many demands on your time that this mistake is especially easy to make...and overlook. You will also learn how an investment of as little as $5 can significantly enhance the way your business is seen by potential clients. It's an investment that is well worth making once you know where to make it.

The tenth chapter addresses what could easily be the single most destructive mistake when it comes to quickly filling your coaching practice...especially when it comes to that new opening created by a client who finishing up their coaching cycle with you. This mistake can cost you weeks of time and effort. The solution presented in this chapter could have you solving the problem in as little as fifteen minutes each time you want a new client.

Chapter eleven addresses manipulating your potential clients. As a coach, you probably do your best not to manipulate clients but rather help to empower them to make the best possible choices for themselves. While this is a noble aspiration, in this one area of your business, it can be especially deadly. However, done in this particular way your clients will thank you for it!

The twelfth chapter is the other chapter that you do not want to skip. The cost to your business of ignoring the information in this chapter can be...well, beyond words. The loss associated with this mistake could remove your business from the internet in a way that is unrecoverable. Your business records are possibly even more vulnerable than your website. This chapter shows several different ways to minimize this risk and save your business should the worst happen. One of my personal friends had her businesses devastated by this mistake while I was writing this book. Read and follow the advice in this chapter so you have a fighting chance against this mistake. The life of your business could depend upon it.

Biggest Topic Mistake

As a coach, especially as you are starting your business, the mistakes addressed in this book may not even be on your radar. You may not even think of them as mistakes, and almost certainly don't have a feeling for the impact they can have on your coaching business.

If you are currently earning a living, or are working toward earning a living as a coaching professional then this book is for you. Every one of these mistakes falls into the realm of "professionalism" in one way or another. Professionalism in terms of how you appear to a customer. Professionalism in how you run your business. Professionalism in how you market your business effectively. Professionalism in how you protect your business from harm and against disaster.

Why This Topic Is Important

The content of this book is not to be taken lightly. On the surface having a "social media strategy," or lack thereof, may not appear to affect you and your business. It actually should be an integral part of the one thing you should be doing every day – marketing your business. If you are not marketing your business every day, even in some small way, then you and your business will never thrive in the way that you could.

What This All Means To You, To Your Life, And To Your Business

That open hour that you see as an opportunity for some "down time" now that your previous client has finished their coaching cycle with you, is actually costing you money. If you had been marketing your business in some way every day, then a simple phone call or email to one of the people on your waiting list could have put several hundred dollars more into your pocket today.

With proper and effective marketing, your coaching business can be filled with your ideal clients. These are the people you love to work with, and help them change their lives for the better in ways that they may never have even imagined before they met you...and hired you to coach them. Your relationship with these wonderful clients is a direct result of your professionalism in every aspect of your business. You owe it to yourself, and your clients, to build a thriving coaching practice by avoiding these 12 dangerous mistakes.

Chapter 1: Look Mommy, I made a website!

What is the mistake?

Having a website that does not look professional is a big mistake. But trying to "speak to everyone" about the processes and services you offer, rather than talking to just your ideal client using their languaging can result in driving your potential clients away. It's also very easy to make so many other seemingly small but critical mistakes. Things like poor layout, bad graphics, too much irrelevant content, confusing menus, and even hosting your website someplace like wordpress.com all send the wrong message about you and your coaching business.

Why is it a mistake?

A potential client who visits your website is looking for relief from some pain in their life or a solution to a problem that they have. They want you to prove to them, through your website, that you are THE person who can help them. When they explore your website they are searching for proof that you are the person they should hire because you understand their issue.

They are searching for a feeling that will lead them to starting a dialogue with you on their way to hiring you. Describing the processes you may use to help them is also a mistake. It is likely to leave them emotionally flat, especially because they don't really care about which processes you may use to help them. They just want to know that you can help them because they found the right words and feelings from your website.

However, if they find a website which leaves them emotionally flat, wondering what you could possibly have to offer them that would help, and are so confused by your menus that they can't even figure out how to contact you, there is no doubt that they will leave your site and never return. You only get one chance to make a first impression with your website! And to make matters worse, they will only invest about six seconds of their precious time to decide whether to stay and look around or to leave your site and never return.

What are the consequences of making this mistake and how critical are they?

In those first few seconds they will decide the fate of their budding relationship with you. You may be exactly the person they are looking for with exactly the right tools, techniques, and experience to quickly and easily help them. But if you don't communicate that to them quickly and effectively in words that they "get" you both lose.

You may have lots of great processes and techniques that you want to highlight on your website. However it is likely that the consequence of using them as menu names will be confusion and frustration, rather than a clear understanding and intuitive navigation around your site.

Describing the processes, tools, and techniques you use in your coaching practice, rather than focusing on the outcome and benefits of coaching with you, will leave a client unimpressed and heading for the door. Your message and your language needs to resonate with your potential client in a way that grabs their attention and lets them know "you are the one!" or you may never even know they considered working with you.

Websites of successful coaching professionals have a certain look and feel about them that instills confidence, and part of that feeling is derived from the layout and color scheme used. Bright pink and green may be great colors for a children's book author's website, but probably not for a professional coach's site.

You can enhance your credibility by having your own domain that describes your business like **ExecutiveCoachAlex.com**. The consequences of not have your own domain, but rather choosing to host your website someplace else is that you end up with a piggyback URL like

ExecutiveCoachAlex.WordPress.com or **home.comcast.net/~ExecutiveCoachAlex**, and that can destroys your credibility in your clients eyes. Amateurs and hobbyists piggyback on other domains; professionals use their own business domain.

Why and when do people tend to make this mistake?

Coaches tend to make these kinds of mistakes for a number of reasons. Many times you will simply get caught up in what you have to offer - the wonderful tools, techniques, and the skills that you bring - and you will lose sight of it really being all about connecting with the client. It's a good bet that your new potential client has no understanding of your coaching tools and techniques, and really doesn't care what they are called...at all! They want to know that you have a proven process that can help them get past their issue and on to living the life they desire.

Your natural tendency as a coach (and a human!) is to use your own languaging to describe things. When someone is looking to hire a coaching professional to help them, what they want to hear, or read, or see, is that you "get them" and are using their words (not yours) to describe their pain, and their issue. As coaches and business owners, we often forget to take that approach until it is pointed out to us. It is not a natural way for us to think, even if it may be natural for a marketing professional. However, we must speak to the potential client in their language if we expect to maximize our engagement with them.

What should they do instead?

Instead of making these mistakes, and many more, we should take some time to learn more about who our ideal client would be and "what makes them tick." Who are they? Where do the live? What do they do for work, and for fun? What are their motivations, their experiences, their challenges, their gifts, and their pain? These are all part of the set of questions you should answer in order to create an Ideal Client Avatar. Give your Ideal Client Avatar a name, and build a biography for them. Find a photo that can represent that person so that you can really "look them in the eye" when you are "speaking to them" as you create your website content and marketing messages.

I like to call my Ideal Client Avatar "FRED." FRED is an acronym that reminds me that Fred Represents Exact Demographics of my idea customer. Your job, in marketing your coaching business, is to "get inside of FRED's head" and understand him as much as you can. That way you can speak to him in ways that truly resonate with him, grab his attention, and will have him hanging on your every word because he KNOWS you understand him, and his pain, and his problems.

Whenever you create anything that you hope will be seen by your ideal client, always create it as if you are talking directly to your Ideal Client Avatar. That avatar should be treated as if they are an individual person who is sitting across the desk from you. You are not speaking to a group; you are speaking to that one person.

Before you become concerned that you are narrowing your focus too far, remember that people will still connect with a message even if is not exactly 100% right on for them. Even if they only resonate with 60%, 70%, or 80% of the message, that is so far beyond the typical 20%-30% connection they make with the typical marketing. So speak directly to your Ideal Client Avatar and the "overlap" from your targeted message will resonate with other people who are close enough to your ideal client for your message to grab their attention too.

It is from this place of understanding the person your Ideal Client Avatar represents that you should start to create your website and marketing messages for maximum effectiveness. Personally, I prefer to work with my ideal client rather than just any old client. Sure their money pays the bills the same way, but one is a whole lot more fun and motivating to work with over the long haul. So speak to the one you would rather work with, and fill your coaching practice with clients like them.

Chapter 1

What should you do if you've already made this mistake? How do you fix it?

You may have recognized a number of mistakes you are making or made before reading this. That's OK. This is probably the first time anyone has ever explained these things to you in this way. It's not your fault for making those mistakes in the past. You simply didn't have the information to take better action.

Your opportunity now is to go back and fix any that you have made. Do so in a way that really supports the growth of your business and speaks directly to your Ideal Client Avatar. Get inside their head and get to know them as well as you know your best friend, because they will be your best friend in business!

When you look at the clients you have attracted, and the effort you had to put into attracting them before learning this, and compare it with your new results using this material, I'm sure you will be pleasantly surprised. It may seem scary at first not to try to get everybody (or just anybody) as a client. However once you start landing more and more of your ideal clients because they recognize you are speaking directly to them in their language, your coaching business, your job satisfaction, and your income will all increase dramatically.

How do we prevent making this mistake moving forward?

The best way to prevent making this mistake moving forward is to take a moment and review everything you do through the eyes of your Ideal Client Avatar. Would that person see it as "professional" and in a way that would resonate with them? Does it communicate that you understand them, their pain, and their wants and desires?

Those are the kinds of questions you will want answers to so you can effectively evaluate what you are doing. It is by viewing it through those eyes that you can ensure that you are being most effective in marketing to your ideal client with your website and beyond.

Any tools or insight to help people get results faster, easier, more efficiently?

Write up a detailed biography of your Ideal Client Avatar and find a picture to represent them. Create a document that has all of that information in one place. Every time you are going to create anything that a potential client would see, read through that Bio first. You want their viewpoint deeply embedded in your "marketing thinking" so you can speak directly to them effortlessly.

What is one BIG piece of advice or "The Key" to avoiding this mistake in the future?

My best piece of advice is that your business will thrive when you speak directly to your Ideal

Customer about their struggles and can prove to them that not only do you understand them and their situation but you do so in their language from a professional looking website. Creating and speaking directly to your Ideal Customer Avatar will clearly and effectively guide you down that path. Having a professional looking website will entice them to stay long enough to actually read your message.

Summary:

- Your website will be judged in the first six seconds by a visitor. Based on what they find there, they will decide to leave or stay a little longer. Having an attractive, professional looking website is critical to making it past those first six seconds.

- Your potential clients are looking for a solution to their problem or pain. If they can't immediately tell that you understand their issue and believe that you might be able to help them, they will leave your website and likely never return.

- Creating your Ideal Client Avatar is the best investment of time and effort you can make in order to set yourself up to be able to effectively speak to your potential customer and turn them into a paying coaching client.

- Determine your FRED and then get inside their head. Get to know them like your best friend, because they are your best friend when it comes to marketing your business.

- In order to get the best possible results from every "marketing message" you put in front of a potential customer, evaluate that message through the eyes of your Ideal Client Avatar. Only then can you know if it's any good. Your website is likely to be the place of first contact with a potential new client. Make it your first stop for evaluation and upgrade.

Chapter 2: My ideal clients abhor Social Media. Besides, I've got a blog!

What is the mistake?

Thinking that you can completely ignore having a social media presence for your coaching business is a serious mistake. Back before Facebook became the 800 pound gorilla that it is in today's social media landscape, having a blog with the ability to leave comments may have been enough.

Why is it a mistake?

Facebook has forever changed the face of social media and the way that people not only engage with their friends and family, but it has also changed the way that we interact with businesses as well. Ignoring the power and reach of a Facebook

"Share" immediately limits your reach to those with whom you can directly communicate. Making that mistake can also limit how quickly your coaching business is filled and how fast it grows.

What are the consequences of making this mistake and how critical are they?

Social media has massively sped up the spread of "viral videos" and other "viral content." While you may think that most "viral content" has something to do with cute animals or someone doing outrageously dangerous or stupid things, that would actually be overlooking the huge opportunity that is waiting there for your business.

The number of inspirational "Memes" and solid content, like TED talks, that get shared every day through social media is substantial. And those are the type of content that are far more likely to attract the type of person who would be interested in coaching with you than a video that starts out with, "Hey Bubba, hold my beer while I show you a cool new trick...."

Ignoring social media to help spread the word of what you have to offer is a mistake that will definitely limit the potential success of your coaching business. Not only will you be reaching more of your potential ideal clients using social media, but you will be building your visibility and authority as a coach in your market as well. You will also be planting seeds of content that can be shared far beyond the limits of your other marketing strategies, and that content can lead new clients back to you.

Why and when do people tend to make this mistake?

Coaches tend to ignore actively using Social Media to promote their business because they often only consider it in terms of advertising on social media sites. While placing ads which are targeted to the specific demographic and interests of your ideal client is a good solid strategy that is not the only way to approach social media.

There can also be a fear that engaging in social media for your business can become a giant time-sink with little return on the time you invest. While that is certainly possible, it doesn't have to be that way if you have a social media strategy and stick to it rather than getting sucked into viewing the newsfeed or other activities unrelated to your plan.

What should they do instead?

Your coaching business should not only have a social media strategy that includes a Facebook business page, but you should also be engaging with current and potential clients on a regular basis. Tying your blog and social media accounts together should be part of that strategy. That way you can make the best use of content you share in either place. You can use social media posts to not only inform, but to help drive visitors to your website where they can "learn more" about that particular topic, as well as you and your coaching business. Having social media sharing buttons on your blog will increase your social media footprint, and the number of people who see your content.

Coordinate your blog and social media content posts so that they naturally cross pollenate each other. Make sure that your posts include at least a call to action to visit your blog and/or LIKE this post somewhere in the content.

Be sure to set up your business page with a vanity URL by claiming it today if you haven't already. Using the name of your business, website, or your name followed by "coaching," are all approaches that could be used. The idea is to have your social media and website URLs related to each other so there is an obvious connection. For example, `http://Facebook.com/WithEFTTapping` is the Facebook "vanity URL" that is associated with my website `http://WithEFTtapping.com`. (Notice that you can use upper case and lower case letters in your vanity URL. Make careful choices from the beginning because you probably will not be able to change it later. I now wish that I had made the "T" in "tapping" lower case in my Facebook vanity URL so it's easier to read.

If another person has already claimed the vanity URL with your name, try adding a middle initial or other variation. Be careful about including a geographic location in the vanity URL though, because that could limit your reach and might cause trouble or confusion if you ever move your business to another location.

Side note: You can mix upper and lower case letters in your main URL to make it easier to read. However, everything after the "/" (as in .com/) is case sensitive, so be sure to take care with that section. For example, "WithEFTtapping.com" and "withefttapping.com" will provide identical results when typed into your browser. However, "WithEFTtapping.com/eft-quick-start-video-learning-system" and "WithEFTtapping.com/EFT-Quick-Start-Video-Learning-System" may not get you to the identical place every time, so be careful with capitalization after the first "forward-slash" in a URL. In this case, my WordPress installation is "fixing" it and they do. However other websites may not be configured to do so, and you could end up on an error page instead.

What should you do if you've already made this mistake? How do you fix it?

If you don't already have a social media presence, start one. At the same time create your social media strategy so that you can use social media engagement, as well as your time cultivating it, effectively. Having a plan to follow, including types of posts, promotions, and free offers to use to help build your social media engagement and your email list, are all things to consider when creating your social media plan.

If you'd like to know more about how to build a social media marketing plan, then be sign up at `http://www.CoachesMarketingToolbox.com/book`. So join now and make sure you get the latest news and information I have to share.

How do we prevent making this mistake moving forward?

Creating and using a social media plan will also help to prevent "dry spells" and lost time as you engage in social media. By knowing what you are planning on doing before you open the social media site in your browser, you can get in, get the tasks accomplished and get back out successfully without falling into the social media newsfeed distraction trap.

Any tools or insight to help people get results faster, easier, more efficiently?

Having your content pre-written before you open the site speeds things up as well because you can simply cut, past & post your content and move on to the next thing on your social media strategy checklist.

What is one BIG piece of advice or "The Key" to avoiding this mistake in the future?

Tracking the direct return on investment for promoting your coaching business through social media may be challenging. However, if you engage with even one new customer who you would not have reached otherwise then every dollar they spend with you comes as a direct result of that social media engagement. Even better is the fact that you get to count their "lifetime customer value," not just the first product or service they buy or session they book with you! That can add up to thousands of dollars from one customer over their time with you. Wouldn't that be a nice ROI for your social media engagement?

Summary:

- Facebook is the 800 pound social media gorilla and should not be ignored if you want to reach more potential new clients and grow your business faster.

- Social Media has a re-sharing aspect to it that gives you a reach beyond what you would otherwise have. Take advantage of that capability by creating and posting engaging content that has "high-sharability" like quizzes, surveys, photo-memes, and videos.

- Secure your business vanity URL and start engaging in marketing your coaching business through social media sharing of valuable content. Establish yourself as someone who shares great content that others will want to re-share so you can take advantage of the viral nature of social media content.

- Building a social media plan for the content you share and the frequency of posting can help minimize the social media distraction factor, and turn it into a workhorse instead.

- Pre-configure the content you will be sharing before you open the site in your browser. That way you can get in, get the job done, and get back out quickly and be less likely to fall into the social media newsfeed distraction trap.

Chapter 3:
CoachFluffyBunny@AOL.com

What is the mistake?

Using an email address like `CoachFluffy` `Bunny@AOL.com` is a mistake that could be very detrimental to your business. This is especially true when trying to attracting new clients who have no kind of relationship with you. Plus, there are actually at least two mistakes that are demonstrated by that email address.

Why is it a mistake?

Part of what makes you attractive as a coach is the degree of professionalism you exhibit in all things that a customer could see. Your email address will be seen by your customers, especially when you include it in your autoresponder messages, on your website, and business cards. The email name (`CoachFluffyBunny`) and the domain

(@**AOL.com**) would both be considered "unprofessional" in this case. Your email domain should match your website domain in order to look like a "real" professional company.

On a personal note, with as many emails as I get every day that have a deceptively labeled "from" address, I tend to be very cautious about opening messages from senders I don't recognize. I always hover the cursor over the "from address" on any messages that are suspicious. If they don't look legitimate, I simply delete them without actually viewing their contents. More than once I've been ready to delete a message but when I checked, I found it was a legitimate message even though I didn't recognize the sender initially. Your customers may not go to that much trouble, and your messages could simply be deleted, unread, if you don't use a professional looking email address.

What are the consequences of making this mistake and how critical are they?

You only have one chance to make a first impression and there are actually several first impressions that you have an opportunity to make. The first time they visit your website, visit your blog, see your opt-in "ethical bribe," see your videos on your website, watch your videos on YouTube, see your email address on your website or in a message from your autoresponder, all carry a "first time" opportunity to shine. Be sure that each of these is consistently high quality and you will not only put your potential new clients at ease, but are likely to attract many more as well.

Why and when do people tend to make this mistake?

Often times we have been using an email address for so long we don't give a second thought to how it might appear to a new customer. In addition, most coaches (especially ones getting established and in the initial stages of building their business) forget that they can have, and should have, more than one email address as part of their business. Part of your professional appearance is at least appearing to have a "staff" as would be indicated by your business having multiple email addresses. This also enables you to "bucket" things so they are easier to keep track of in the long run.

What should they do instead?

The very first email addresses you should create for your business are:

- **YourName@YourBusiness.com**
- **Support@YourBusiness.com**
- **Postmaster@YourBusiness.com**

While the purposes of the first two are obvious, the third one needs an explanation. There are some email services (and companies) who will reject emails (and consider them as Spam) if it is not possible to contact Postmaster@YourBusiness.com. So if you want your emails to have the highest possible chance of actually making it to their intended destination, be sure to create the Postmaster email account too.

While this appears to mean that you will now have at least three additional email addresses to check for messages, that doesn't actually have to be the case. Most, if not all, email hosting services (including the ones associated with website hosting) have a way to automatically forward incoming emails to another email address. This enables you to only have to check one business email account.

A word of caution: If you decide to forward all of your business email to your personal email account so that then you really only have to check one email account, be aware of a problem that can create. When you reply to a business email from your personal account, the message will be delivered to the recipient as coming from your personal account. Not only could that cause confusion (and potential embarrassment depending upon the name on the sending email account) but it doesn't look professional.

As a result, it is probably best to keep your business and personal email separate. Sure, you can have them both open at the same time, in separate tabs in a browser for example. But remember to always send business emails from your business email account in order to maintain the professional appearance.

What should you do if you've already made this mistake? How do you fix it?

If you're already using a single email address for everything, it's not too late. Create the recommended new email accounts and start using them. Use them for correspondence as well as on your website, videos, business cards, marketing material, and social media, at a minimum.

Depending upon which tools you use with your personal email, there may be a way to set up a "filter" that would either A) sort all "business & client email" into a separate folder, and/or B) automatically forward that email to your business email account.

Be sure to start publicizing your new business email address when responding to client emails. It would also be a good idea to send out a broadcast email to all of your clients saying that you are "upgrading your service" and have a new business email account that you would like them to use moving forward.

How do we prevent making this mistake moving forward?

The only way to prevent making this mistake is make the investment of time, effort, and money to upgrade your business resources, and appearance, and actually start using these new email addresses. It's not complicated to do, but it does have to be done before you can start using them.

Any tools or insight to help people get results faster, easier, more efficiently?

With every website hosting plan that I know about, there is an option (usually free) to have at least a handful of email addresses associated with that website domain. You already have access, so make use of that service.

Your web hosting company likely has online tutorials that show how to set up an email address associated with your domain.

YouTube is another place to search for a video tutorial on how to set up an email account for your domain on your web hosting service.

Your web hosting service's help desk definitely can help you and point you to information on how to accomplish setting up those email accounts.

When it comes to your personal business email account, you could use

- `Firstname@YourBusiness.com`
- `Firstname.Lastname@YourBusiness.com`

The second may be preferred in case you ever have a team member join your business who has the same first name. You might as well plan for the future growth of your business to those levels while it's a minor tweak during setup.

Be sure to use capital letters in your email address and domain name to make them easier to read. Upper case letters will automatically be converted to lower case by the email or web software, but to a human it really helps with readability if they start out as mixed upper and lower case.

What is one BIG piece of advice or "The Key" to avoiding this mistake in the future?

My best advice is to make today the day to correct this mistake. Your business success depends upon your professional appearance, and this is one way to quickly and easily upgrade that appearance. You can't change what happened in the past, but you can improve the future by setting up your professional business email accounts.

Summary:

- `YourName@YourBusiness.com` should be your primary business email address.

- Also create `Support@YourBusiness.com` and `Postmaster@YourBusiness.com` for best efficiency and email delivery.

- You can set it up to auto forward multiple email accounts to one account so that you can read all of your business email there.

- Remember to think about which account you are sending your reply emails out from. If it's your personal account, you could be sending the message to your potential new client from

- **CoachFluffyBunny@AOL.com** instead of **YourName@YourBusiness.com** or **Support@YourBusiness.com**

Chapter 4: I found it free on the internet so I can use it... right?

What is the mistake?

Not paying attention to copyrights and terms of service can not only get you in trouble, it can cost you a lot of extra money. It's not just the lawyer's fees, but also the surprise bills for using the copyrighted material that can add up very quickly.

Another big mistake that seriously exposes your business to legal risk is to take the position, "everyone else is doing it...so I will too." Your mama was right about this one when she said, "If everyone else was jumping off of a cliff, would that be a smart move for you too?" Enough said.

Why is it a mistake?

It is definitely a mistake to think that anything you find on the internet that is not obviously marked with a copyright is freely available for use by you and anyone else. There are at least four problems hiding within that thinking that can get you into expensive trouble.

The first mistake is thinking that you can use anything without an obvious copyright. The second is thinking that it doesn't matter where you acquire it. The third mistake is not having proof of where you acquired the license for it. The fourth mistake is thinking that if you "create a derivative work" from it, you will be in the clear.

What are the consequences of making this mistake and how critical are they?

If you take someone's copyrighted material, it could be a photo, a video, music, or even regular every day text, and use it for your own purposes without permission, you are infringing on the rights of the copyright holder. This can get very expensive to fix.

Two different friends of mine got "tagged" by the copyright holder, in both cases Getty Images, for $1500 in one case and $4000 in the other. There have been lots of comments that I've seen about how aggressively Getty Images is about protecting the copyrights the whole. One of those friends had the image up on her website for less than 24 hours and took it down because she didn't like the image. The second had his Virtual Assistant setup the website and the VA did not "properly" source the image.

I also have a friend who is a professional nature photographer who regularly sends bills for $500 or more to people for using her images which they have stolen from her website. Some of these unscrupulous characters even go so far as to "erase" her copyright notice watermark from the images. Others are using them without a license and printing them as calendars and making money off of her work without compensating her in any way.

Sometimes the people she sends bills to will write back and say, "...but I got it off of a "royalty free" image site..." and then reference one of those sites where anybody can upload photos and "claim" they are royalty free. Those are the type of sites that I stay away from for exactly that reason.

Why and when do people tend to make this mistake?

People tend to make this mistake for several reasons. The first and probably the most common is that they don't really have much of an understanding of copyrights, and may think they apply only to written work, or "copy."

Another common mistake is not reading the terms of service for the sites where you find the image (or music, or video, or text) you want to use. Some of these sites, like iStockPhoto and others, offer to sell licenses for the use of "royalty free" images, video, or music.

When you purchase one of those licenses, you are generally granted a non-exclusive license to use that image (or other copyrighted work) in the ways that are described within the license terms of service. This license may include terms about using the image as-is, or as part of a derivative or composite work. The ways and places that the image can be used are covered as well, including such uses as online, for commercial purposes, for educational purposes, or for offline and physical reproduction or printing of the images. There are generally different licenses (and license costs) that cover higher volume usage, and rendering those images into physical medium, like a poster, calendar, book, or coffee cup, etc.

It can seem a bit complex from this explanation, but it is very important to stay within the license terms if you don't like unexpected, and potentially expensive, nasty-surprises.

It is important to understand what kind of "image site" you are visiting. Sites where you are purchasing a license to use an image have obvious terms of service and license agreements that make your rights clear. It is best to review the license terms before purchasing any copyrighted material for use. In addition, I have found that the same image will often be available from several such sources, but that the license terms are different, as are the costs. So check around and see what works best for you.

In contrast, there are other "image sites" that offer images for use without charge, and those are the ones where you really need to look further before you use those images. Some of those "free" sites are nothing more than image sharing sites where the only "copyright control" is to have the person who is uploading the image "check a box" saying that they have the rights to share the image with others. That is completely different from the copyright holder consciously placing an image in the public domain for anyone to use. The terms of service (TOS) for these sites often try to remove themselves from the whole copyright question by placing the burden on the person uploading the image and/or downloading it for use.

There are both "free" (unlicensed) and "royalty free" licensing sites for video and audio as well. The same arguments and problems discussed for images apply to these sites, as do the copyright issues that need to be addressed.

So if you want to stay out of trouble, know where your images, videos, and audios are coming from and make sure you keep a copy of your receipt and any terms of service and/or license agreement associated with any media you acquire.

There is another class of images (and videos, audios, and text) that can be very useful. Those are images which are in the public domain. There are many sites out there where you can find public domain images, and it is often very clear from the information on those sites that the images are in the public domain. Many US Government sites have information which is in the public domain, but you should still make sure to check the TOS for the site. You are the one who will pay for any mistakes, so take a moment to confirm it. Information on state and local government sites may or may not be in the public domain, so don't get caught off guard by thinking it is a "government site" so it is public domain. Always check, especially in the beginning before you really understand the rules.

Outside of the USA you will need to make sure you understand the rules that apply not only for your country, but the country from which you are sourcing the copyrighted material. It can get quite complicated quickly because of all of the laws and rules involved.

In general, you are better off purchasing a license to use the copyrighted material, and keeping proof of the purchase along with the license and terms of service, just in case there is ever a question. This is definitely a case where "an ounce of prevention is worth way more than a pound of cure!"

What should they do instead?

The first thing you should do is learn more about copyrights by visiting
`http://www.copyright.gov/help/faq/faq-general.html`

This FAQ has relatively short answers for a number of questions including:

Chapter 4

- What is a copyright?
- What does a copyright protect?
- When is my work protected?

An understanding of the answers to these three basic questions will get you started, and help keep you out of trouble.

To summarize <u>my understanding</u> from reading that site (this is NOT legal advice):

- A work has copyright protection from the moment it is created and fixed in a tangible form that can be perceived either with or without the aid of a device or machine. Copyrights cover both unpublished and published works, and protect original works of authorship. It covers a wide variety of authorship, including literary works, music, dramatic works, as well as artistic works such as movies, songs, computer software, poetry, novels, and even architecture.
- It should be noted that while "works" are copyrighted, some things like facts, ideas, and systems, are not copyrighted in and of themselves. However, the way that they are expressed may be copyrighted (as printed material for example.)
- Copyrights are different from trademarks and patents, each of which have their own rules and regulations.

As you can see, this is getting complicated in a hurry. It is best to spend a few minutes exploring the copyright.gov website so you have an understanding for yourself.

What should you do if you've already made this mistake? How do you fix it?

If you realize (or even wonder) if you are infringing on someone else's copyright, your best course of action is to seek legal counsel regarding the situation. You might even want to consider taking it down, or removing it from your website even before you talk to your lawyer and have a better understanding of the situation. I'm not a lawyer, and I don't even play one on TV, so I'm definitely not qualified to suggest any course of action beyond seeking counsel from a qualified professional.

It could also be an expensive mistake to "hope" your infringement will go unnoticed and that you won't get a "cease and desist" letter in the mail. That's not a prudent business position to take, and you are in business as a coach.

Another secondary mistake which is easier to fix is not keeping your documentation in order. If you know that you have purchased a license, go back and find it (and your proof of payment) and get copies of the license agreement and TOS. Then keep them all in one location where you can quickly and easily find them should you ever need to do so.

Do it now before you have a disk crash and lose all of your email or other proof. Don't rely on your ability to remember where each and every piece of licensed material came from.

How do we prevent making this mistake moving forward?

Moving forward, the best tactic for avoiding this mistake is to always know exactly where your copyrightable assets came from, and have proof of license, or proof that it is in the public domain, or that you otherwise have a legal right to use that material.

Gather and organize your proof of license and payment, as well as TOS & license terms and add them to your permanent business records every time you acquire a new licensed (or public domain) work. You may never need them, but if you do, it will definitely lower your stress level to have it all organized and available where you can easily find it.

Any tools or insight to help people get results faster, easier, more efficiently?

One of my favorite royalty free image sites is PresenterMedia. I have been using images from them on my website and in PowerPoint videos for several years. I've arranged for a special offer for my readers. You can learn more about it by visiting `http://CoachesMarketingToolbox.com/media`. I especially like PresenterMedia because they not only have images available for use, but also PowerPoint templates and animations, as well as presentation clipart, and video backgrounds. Many of their clipart items can be customize by changing the color and/or the text before downloading them. That can greatly lessen the need to modify the graphic beyond resizing it to fit your particular use.

Another site where I will often purchase royalty free images is iStockPhoto. When I'm looking for a specific image I will look on iStockPhoto first. They have a wide variety of images available and some of them are exclusive to iStockPhoto. I have also arranged for a special offer from iStockPhoto for my readers. You can learn more about it by visiting: **http://CoachesMarketingToolbox.com/media**.

When I'm looking to license royalty free audio or video clips I will start my search at VideoBlocks. Not only do they have a variety of video clips, including regular, time lapse, and slow motion, but they also have production music and sound effect clips as well. They also have an "effects" category than can be useful when creating "lower thirds" (the names & titles you see on the news for example.) They also offer Adobe After Effects templates that can be used to create some stunning intro and outro clips to use as bookends for your videos.

I have also arranged for a special offer from VideoBlocks for my readers. You can learn more about it by visiting: **http://CoachesMarketingToolbox.com/media**. All of the media related resources and special offers can be found on this page.

Chapter 4

What is one BIG piece of advice or "The Key" to avoiding this mistake in the future?

Do not rely on others, like a VA or outsourcer, to remember to watch out for this (or even care about it!) It is likely that they also do not have much of an understanding of copyright rules and could inadvertently (through carelessness, laziness, or just plain being too busy) put your business in jeopardy. If you are outsourcing any graphic work, be sure that you specify either that you are providing all base images, or that the work created must be 100% original, AND that they are transferring copyright (or a license) to you as part of the job. That also goes for other forms of copyrightable material – Video, Audio, Text, etc.

Summary:

- Ignoring copyrights can be expensive and dangerous to your businesses finances and your stress level should you ever run into trouble.

- Understanding a little bit about copyrights up front will save you hours of work, and loads of money trying to fix the problem later.

- A basic understanding of copyrights may be enough to guide you down the path and minimize the risk for you and your business because you will know how and where to look to acquire licensed or public domain material.

- Keeping good records of the source of any licensed (or public domain) material along with the Terms Of Service and license conditions will prove invaluable to your business if there is ever a legal question about your rights.

Chapter 5: I'm coaching them; they don't really care what I look like!

What is the mistake?

Hiding behind your website, telephone, and Skype connection and never providing your clients with a picture of you is a mistake that can drive away clients. People want to know not only about how you can help them through coaching, but they want to know what you look like as part of establishing a relationship with you.

Why is it a mistake?

Not having a photo or video of yourself on your website is a mistake because you are building a relationship with your customers. That relationship is likely to include some intimate details of their life, so they want to know that you are someone they can trust. As we all know, we gather lots of clues about someone from the way they look and the way they present themselves. Our level of trust is at least partially based on the visual clues we find. When we find none, we tend to ask the question, "What are they hiding?" That's obviously not the best way to start a coaching relationship.

What are the consequences of making this mistake and how critical are they?

If you, personally, aren't visible enough on your website and in your marketing, it is very likely that some of your ideal customers will slip away never having contacted you. They are looking for the right person to coach them, and part of being the "right person" can only be determined through a subjective feel that starts with an image and a voice. Be sure you are including both of those in your marketing material and on your website.

Part of "your voice" is the way you communicate through the words, images, and videos on your website. You may have audio recordings available there too. Some coaches include an audio or video Welcome Messages that help establish who they are in the eyes of their potential clients. While it is not unusual for a welcome video to auto play when your website first loads, it would be more courteous to not do so in case they are visiting your website from work and don't want to have your website audibly advertise that fact.

Why and when do people tend to make this mistake?

It is easy to overlook having your photo on your website if your photo is not part of the website header. You have likely been very focused on making sure your website layout looks good and the text content is the best possible representation of what you have to offer your potential clients. So you may not remember to add a photo of yourself to your About page at a minimum.

Another common reason that your photo never quite makes it onto your website is because you don't have a current professional photo. You are likely very correct in thinking that a Selfie from your smartphone isn't the best option to show you in a professional light to a potential new client.

What should they do instead?

If you don't have a good photo to use on your website, then invest in yourself and your business by having some professional photos taken. We are not talking photos from the Sears or Walmart photo studio here! It may cost more, but the results will be better when you hire a professional photographer.

Make an "Introduction and welcome to my website" video that you can use on the front page of your website. Not only will this give your potential clients a much better feeling for who you are and what you have to offer, but it can elevate your professionalism in their eyes as well.

What should you do if you've already made this mistake? How do you fix it?

If you have made the mistake of not having "you" on your website, be sure to fix that by adding a photo at the very least. Adding a welcome video should be your next step.

If your photos are "old" be sure to update them and keep them current. Things like major hair style, length, or color changes are excellent opportunities for new photos. Significant weight changes that would be obvious in the photos are another one, although we may not feel as good about those depending upon the direction of the change. Those are each an important reasons to make a change.

One internet marketing "coach" I was following updated her photo and it appeared that she'd jumped about 15+ years in age. I was not impressed and felt that she had been misrepresenting herself for most of the time I had been following her. I wondered what else was she hiding or misrepresenting. As a result, her credibility came into question in my mind, and I wondered about the accuracy and validity of everything she said for quite a while after that change. Had I met her in person before seeing the new photos, my trust would have been damaged even further. Don't make that same mistake. It's not worth the potential damage to your relationship with your potential clients.

How do we prevent making this mistake moving forward?

The only way to prevent this mistake moving forward is to fix it now. And once you do have your current photos and videos on your website, be sure to schedule a review date on your calendar for every 6 months or so. Hairstyles change, and you want to be reviewing your website on a regular basis anyway, so this is a good time to add it to your schedule.

Any tools or insight to help people get results faster, easier, more efficiently?

Whenever you hire someone to create a photo, video, or audio for you, remember to discuss copyrights. Are you receiving the copyright to the work, or are you simply receiving a license for the work.

Also make sure you have some kind of Work For Hire agreement in place that explicitly spells out the copyright issue, and services provided, so that you are not left wondering or find yourself in trouble later. Understand if you will receive the "raw" images, or video, or if they will have been enhanced, edited, and processed into a finished product.

What is one BIG piece of advice or "The Key" to avoiding this mistake in the future?

Videos can be expensive to have professionally made. The good news is that YouTube has lowered the bar for the quality that is expected for this type of video. While we are all constantly exposed to "high production quality" video on TV and in movies, your potential ideal customer has also been exposed to "low to moderate production quality" videos on YouTube and is likely to be more understanding.

You can learn how to make a good looking welcome video, with good audio quality, and good lighting fairly easily these days. Gone are the days of video production requiring expensive video cameras and a sound stage in order to create a reasonable welcome video. Yes, the quality can go up substantially as a result of investing in that sort of video, but there are alternatives.

I know of several "video gurus" on the internet who are making the vast majority of their high quality videos with an iPhone! Of course they are using a tripod, rather than it being hand-held, and they are using some additional audio equipment and lights, but that's really about it. They have the skill and knowledge to choose a good location and use their minimal equipment effectively. And you can too if you choose to make videos on a regular basis as part of your business content, or marketing. But if you are likely to only make one to a few videos each year, then you are probably better off hiring some help.

As with most technology these days, video production is constantly evolving. You can find my best current advice by visiting:
http://CoachesMarketingToolbox.com/video.

Chapter 5

When it comes to finding a photographer or videographer to hire, one place you can look is Craig's List. Many cities around the world have a local listing area on Craigslist.com. Be sure to ask to see examples of their work before you hire them and get a clear understanding of the services they are offering and the price.

Summary:

- Potential clients who find your photo and a good quality welcome video on your website are more likely to engage in coaching with you because they can see you.

- Professionally created photos and videos bring more of you to your website, and marketing material, and build the Know-Like-Trust factor with your potential client.

- Videos need to have a professional feel to them, and good quality, but they do not need "high production value" as in the movies and on TV. YouTube has lowered the bar to something much more attainable at a reasonable cost.

- If you are not already set up to make good quality videos, hire someone with the right equipment to help you. CraigsList.com can be a good place to start looking for these resources.

Chapter 6:
I'll break the Internet if I do something wrong!

What is the mistake?

Many coaches have a fear that if they get into their WordPress dashboard and start adding or editing things they will irreparably destroy their website. You may even be afraid that website technology is way beyond what you can quickly and easily learn, so you never even attempt to fix something as simple as a typo. This same fear leads to never updating your website, resulting in obviously outdated information being shown to your website visitors.

Why is it a mistake?

We all recognize that the quality of the material we put out is a direct reflection on us and our business. Sometimes typos and errors creep in unnoticed, but when we do notice them we want to be able to correct the mistake. In the eyes of a website visitor, not fixing them reflects poorly on the perceived quality of everything you deliver. Stale and outdated website information sends the message that either you don't care about the content of your website, simply don't pay attention to details and are sloppy about what you do, or may even have gone out of business because the information is so outdated.

What are the consequences of making this mistake and how critical are they?

Typos and errors can be yet another reason for a visitor to leave your website never to return. First time visitors are looking for a reason to cross you off their list of possibilities quickly so they can continue their search elsewhere. They quickly notice things like typos and errors, as well as how current the content is, or at least how recently it was added, based on the post dates. They may see old stale information as an indicator that you're not actively engaged in your business and recruiting new clients, so they will simply move on. The same holds true for sites with comment spam.

Why and when do people tend to make this mistake?

Coaches have been trained in coaching, not website design and maintenance, so it is natural to think "there is unfamiliar complex magic in there somewhere" and avoid looking deeper into what is reasonable and easy to do on your website yourself.

You may have had someone create your website for you and they wanted you to stay out of it so they can continue to charge you a monthly fee for "maintenance and updates." That is not an unreasonable request on their part, since they may have to fix any problems that arise from "you poking around in there" and you would have to pay for that fix too.

What should they do instead?

What most coaches who haven't had any website or WordPress training fail to recognize is that if you can use a word processor, like Microsoft Word, then you probably have the basic skills needed to at least fix typos and make minor updates and additions to your site.

WordPress has multiple "levels of access permission" that help safeguard the content from inadvertent mistakes by users who don't have enough knowledge to "dig in deeper than their pay grade." These "Roles" or access levels are (in descending order of "power over the website") Administrator, Editor, Author, Contributor, and Subscriber.

- Administrators are the ones who have access to everything, from the ability to edit the internal workings of WordPress PHP scripts, on down to viewing the content. They have access to all of the administration functions for the site too.

- Editors have the ability to write, publish, and manage pages and posts including those of other users. Editors can moderate comments and manage links.
- Authors can publish and manage only their own posts.
- Contributors can write and manage their own posts, but they cannot publish the content to make it visible on the site.
- A subscriber can only view and interact with the content on the site, and manage their own account profile.

As the owner of the website you will want to have access in the role of Editor, or at least Author. Because you have the desire to keep your website current, you will need to be able to add new posts, fix typos and errors, and otherwise keep your website content current. For the vast majority of those kinds of needs the roll of Editor (or Author if you don't need to moderate comments) is likely to be sufficient to deal with the content of the website. Those roles provide what is needed to modify the content without having to be concerned about the mechanics that making the site run properly. The Administrator should take care of that part.

Part of the Administrator's roll is to keep the underlying "WordPress engine" running smoothly by testing and installing updates to WordPress itself, along with the updates for plugins and themes. The Administrator should also be ensuring that regular backups of your site are happening correctly and are available if you should ever need them.

The Administrator is also the one who should be in charge of website security. There are a number of enhancements and configuration details that should be put in place in order to minimize the chances of any hackers being able to get into the belly of your website and causing damage. One of these measures is having regular backups. See Chapter 12 for more details.

What should you do if you've already made this mistake? How do you fix it?

If you do not have Editor or Author access to your website, you should ask for it from your Webmaster. That way you can not only fix those typos and keep your calendar up to date, but add fresh content and moderate the comments that come in from new posts.

There are many places where you can learn the basics needed to be able to operate in your new role as Editor or Author. You may even be able to find that information on YouTube. Be sure to check out several videos there as you can never be 100% certain that the information matches your particular WordPress installation and version. They will give you a good start, and you can ask your Webmaster questions from there.

If you'd like to know more about how to use the Editor and Author roles in WordPress, then be sure to sign up over at:

http://www.CoachesMarketingToolbox.com/book. Those are the kind of topics that I plan to cover, and maybe even the one of the topics covered in my next book. So sign up now and make sure you get the latest news and information I have to share.

How do we prevent making this mistake moving forward?

The only way to prevent this mistake from happening moving forward is to have the knowledge and capability available to make the necessary changes. You can have your webmaster make the changes for you, or you can learn what you need to know and do it yourself while still having your webmaster maintain the other areas that are needed to keep your site trouble free and running smoothly.

Any tools or insight to help people get results faster, easier, more efficiently?

Learning all the details of how to "install and run" a WordPress website can seem rather daunting at first. I have invested many hundreds of hours over the last five years or so studying WordPress, how to configure it, what plugins to use, how to use them effectively and all of the other "stuff" that has come along with being my own Webmaster for the handful of sites I own.

Fortunately, you probably have no need for 95% of the information I've gleaned over the years. What you do need, however, is some basic information about how to use WordPress as an Editor or Author. With that in mind, I've put together some resources that can help you get started quickly over at:

`http://www.CoachesMarketingToolbox.com/wp`.
One of the challenging things about WordPress is that it continues to evolve as new releases of the software, plugins and themes are made. As a result, I will be updating the content on a regular basis and as I find new and better resources for you. So be sure to check it out so you can get started quickly.

What is one BIG piece of advice or "The Key" to avoiding this mistake in the future?

One big piece of advice for when you are first start working inside your website with these new capabilities is to NOT delete things. You can move them to the Trash, but do NOT empty the trash or delete what is in the trash for a while...even weeks or months. That way, if you realize that you have made a mistake and have removed something that you didn't intend to, you can more easily recover.

Also, ask your webmaster to make a backup right before you start working in your site for the first time. That way, if things "go badly" you still have a recovery plan to take you back to where you started.

Summary:

- If you can use a word processor like Microsoft Word, then with a little education you can keep your website current and even add content without needing to have your webmaster make the changes for you.

- There are multiple WordPress roles with different access capabilities. For the majority of what you will need to do, having the Editor or Author role is likely sufficient. Have your webmaster set up that access for you.

- Educate yourself on the basics of using WordPress before you start making changes. You may be able to find that information on YouTube. Check out several of the more recent videos as they are more likely to have current information and will be more likely to match your setup.

- Have your webmaster create a backup of your site before you start working with it the first time, as your "insurance policy" for any mistakes you might make.

- Your webmaster should be the one looking after the underlying WordPress software, plugins, and theme updates, as well as site security.

Chapter 7:
Nobody would ever guess...

What is the mistake?

Using a weak password is asking for trouble when it comes to anything that is accessible through the internet. Your email account, your WordPress website administrator account, your website hosting account, your bank account, your investment account, your Facebook account, your Twitter account, and even your account with the local Power Company are all to a greater or lesser degree vulnerable depending upon the strength of your passwords.

Why This Is a Mistake

Sure, a person who doesn't know you would probably never guess your password, but the thing is that hackers aren't people who guess! They use sophisticated software programs that can try thousands upon thousands of "guesses" at your password every second. They start trying to hack into your account by using a list of the most common words that are used as a password, like "password," and do what is called a dictionary search from there. They simply try each and every word on their list, from the simple and more common ones on through the more obscure ones in the dictionary. They will also try number sequences too.

And once they exhaust their dictionary and numeric searches, their software will simply move on to sequentially trying strings of letters and numbers. And at some point they will try upper case letters and symbols too.

In many cases people will only use strings of 4-8 characters to make up their password. At the speed with which computers can try a new guess for your password, it only takes a few moments to try every possible combination. And most of the time, they don't even have to get past the first part of their "commonly used passwords" list before they have cracked your password and have full access to your account.

What are the consequences of making this mistake and how critical are they?

Needless to say, the consequences of making this mistake can be extremely severe. If your password gets cracked by some hackers' computer, then a little bell goes off on some hacker's computer somewhere, and the person running the hack starts looking around to see what interesting information they can steal from you, now that they have full access to your account.

If they have hacked into your Email account, they may also have access to more than enough information to steal your identity or at a minimum send everyone in your address book (including your clients!) a friendly little email about how they can get Viagra at a discount by clicking on this link!

Why and when do people tend to make this mistake?

People make this mistake because they are human, and think like humans instead of computers. Sure, a human may not think to try the name of your favorite puppy from when you were a kid. But to a hacker's software, "rover" is just another word on the list to be tried, and it has no idea of the significance to you of that word – nor does it care!

Another reason people make this mistake is because they have to remember their passwords. And with as many different online accounts as each of us has these days that can add up to having to remember a lot of passwords. This leads to another common password mistake: reuse.

It's likely that you have heard something like, "one account, one password – not twelve accounts, one password!" The idea is that you want to limit the possible damage that a malicious hacker can do by figuring out any one password.

WARNING	If you use the same password for your Email and your bank account, stop right now and go change your bank account password! Do NOT read any further in this book until you have done so!

Now that you have changed your bank account password, you can feel safer, because at least now someone with access to your Email account can't gain easy access to your bank account. That is unless you emailed your bank password to yourself. You didn't do that did you? (You know what to do if you did! Go!)

What should they do instead?

The solution to this problem is to use a strong password, or at least a stronger one than you are using now. There are even some simple tricks that I'll be sharing later that you can start using today.

The obvious question now is, "What makes a strong(er) password?"

A strong(er) password is longer and has more types of characters used in the password. This would include upper case letters, lower case letters, numbers, and special characters or symbols like (~!@#$%^&*_-+=:';",.) for example.

Some systems cannot accept every type of special character that you can type on the keyboard. You should still be sure to use as many different type of characters as possible, regardless of any restrictions.

A common question is, "Why does adding a different type of characters make it harder to guess my password?" In order to answer, we'll have to get into a tiny bit of math.

Let me start with a simple example to help illustrate this point.

Let's assume that you are going to create a password which is only one character in length and you are restricted to the letters "a" – "z". In that case you only have 26 possible passwords. However, you could easily double the number of possible passwords by allowing both lower case and upper case letters.

So if you choose your single character password from "a-z, A-Z" you now have 54 possible choices. And if you then add "0-9" to the possible list, then you have 64 choices. Now if you add these 32 special characters ~`!@#$%^&*-_=+()[] {}\ | ;:' ",.<>/? to the list of possible choices, you now have 86 possibilities to choose from.

Moving from 26 to 86 more than triples the possible choices, but adding more characters to the length of your password actually helps exponentially more. Again, we need a bit of math to help explain.

In this simple example, let's assume for the sake of illustration that you only have 4 possible characters to choose from: A, B, C, and D. With a one character password chosen from this set of 4 possible choices we obviously only have 4 choices, A, B, C, and D.

Now, let's say that we move from a one character password to a two character password. Now we can choose from 16 possible choices: AA, AB, AC, AD, BA, BB, BC, BD, CA, CB, CC, CD, DA, DB, DC, DD. This can be represented mathematically in this way:

$$(NumberOf\ Choices)^{(Length\ Of\ Password)}$$

In this case, there are 4 choices (A, B, C, D) and a length of 2 or 4^2 or 4 x 4 which is 16 possible password.

Now if we move to a 3 character password length, then there are 4^3 or 4 x 4 x 4 or 64 possible passwords.

So every time we add a character to the length we increase the exponent by one and as a result the number of possible passwords increases exponentially.

Now, let's combine the two – more character choices and longer passwords. The table below shows how rapidly the number of password choices increases in each case.

Password	a-z	a-z, A-Z	a-z, A-Z, 0-9	a-z, A-Z, 0-9, Special
Length	26	54	64	86
1	26	54	64	86
2	676	2,916	4,096	7,396
3	17,576	157,464	262,144	636,056
4	456,976	8,503,056	16,777,216	54,700,816
5	11,881,376	459,165,024	1,073,741,824	4,704,270,176
6	308,915,776	24,794,911,296	68,719,476,736	404,567,235,136
7	8,031,810,176	1,338,925,209,984	4,398,046,511,104	4,792,782,221,696
8	208,827,064,576	72,301,961,339,136	281,474,976,710,656	2,992,179,271,065,860

Comparing the bottom line in the table, choosing from all 86 available characters makes it more than 14,000 times harder for a hacker to crack your password when compared to simply using 26 lower case characters. And for each additional character you add to the length of the password, the difficulty increases exponentially.

So the key take-away from this is to use longer passwords and use all four types of available characters (upper and lower case, numbers, and special characters) in your password! And DO NOT use words that you can find in the dictionary.

What should you do if you've already made this mistake? How do you fix it?

There is only one thing to do if you've already made this mistake and that is to systematically go back to every one of your online accounts and change your old password to a new strong(er) password. As long as you get there before your account has been compromised you may be OK. Unfortunately, hackers aren't courteous enough to send you a message saying, "I'm planning on hacking into your account next Tuesday" so you will have no warning about when it will occur. So take care of changing your passwords today!

How do we prevent making this mistake moving forward?

The strongest passwords are made up of a long string of characters chosen at random from all four groups (upper and lower case, numbers, and special characters.)

When I google "Strong Random Password Generator" I find a number of sites including **http://PasswordsGenerator.net** where you can generate a random password and choose which type of characters to include. They also have a nice feature in that by checking a box you can Exclude Similar Characters: (e.g. i, l, o, 1, 0, I) which helps us humans be able to tell which characters are being used without having to guess.

That's great, but how the heck are you supposed to remember something like "AQ@UX/~2XK>8a3P"? (Or phonetically it could be: "APPLE QUEEN @ USA XBOX / ~ 2 XBOX KOREAN > 8 apple 3 PARK " ...as if THAT helps!)

Well the good news is that there are a number of secure password managers with built in random password generation that you can use (more details below.) By using one of these tools, you can have it generate, and remember for you, a more secure password for each site that you visit that requires a password. The beauty of these tools is that now YOU don't have to remember all 37 sixteen-digit-random-character-passwords for the sites which require them. You have a tool to do that for you. And while you may still have to remember one master password, it is a whole lot easier to remember one than a whole handful of passwords.

Any tools or insight to help people get results faster, easier, more efficiently?

So what can you do to increase the security of your passwords if you don't want to go all the way to using a password manager? The answer is character substitution. While it is definitely not nearly as secure as a strong(er) random password, you can still increase the strength by choosing a character substitution set and sticking with it.

There are some obvious substitution possibilities: $ for s, 0 (zero) for o, 1(one) for i, 3 for E, @ for a, & for G, # for H, or 4 for an upside-down h. So using those substitutions, "Whiz-bangs" becomes "W#1z-b@n&$" which at least approaches appearing "random" because of the special character substitutions, and yet if you remember the "key" word, and the character substitutions which are close to obvious, you end up with a stronger password than you would have otherwise.

The down side of substitution is that the hackers are smart, and so they are likely to try dictionary words with common substitutions before they go to full random password testing. No password is ever 100% safe from hacking (which is why I've been saying "strong(er)" password). The only thing that you can do is make it as hard as is reasonably possible for them to guess your password. Longer, non-dictionary words with substitutions are a great start, short of using a password manager.

Password Managers

At the time I'm writing this, there are three password managers that seem to be most widely used in my experience. Each of them has their own quirks and advantages, so you will need to do your own investigation into which one works best for you.

I have gathered my most current recommendations for password managers all in one place for my readers. Technology is constantly changing and so may my recommendations. You can learn more about what I'm recommending today by visiting:
http://CoachesMarketingToolbox.com/passwords

LastPass: Free download for Windows, Mac, Linux, and Mobile devices. There is a premium version at a reasonable cost for some enhanced features. One nice feature of LastPass is that there is a way to share "login information" with another LastPass user (friend, family, or outsource worker.) The password remains hidden and you are able to delete it once the need for sharing that login information has been completed.

RoboForm: Free version (limited number of logins stored) for Windows, Mac, Linux, and some mobile devices. The full version is available at a reasonable price on an annual renewal plan. Like LastPass, RoboForm has a way to securely share specific logins (or Safenotes) using an encrypted transfer option.

1Password: Free version (30 day trial) for PC, Mac, and iOS devices. A single user or family licenses may be purchased. Licenses are a one-time purchase, rather than an annual purchase. Upgrades may be available at no or reduced cost when needed due to feature enhancements or operating system changes that require 1Password updates – see their website for details.

Again, you can get my latest recommendations and links for access by visiting: **http://CoachesMarketingToolbox.com/passwords**

What is one BIG piece of advice or "The Key" to avoiding this mistake in the future?

The PasswordsGenerator.net website recommends the following approaches:

To prevent your password from being hacked with social engineering, brute force or dictionary attack methods:

- Do not use the same password on multiple accounts. One password, one account!

- Use longer passwords (containing at least 15-20 characters) that include numbers, upper and lower case letters, and special symbols.

- Do not use the names of your family, friends, pets, postcodes, house numbers, phone numbers, birthdates, ID card numbers, social security numbers, etc.

- Do not use the most commonly used English words.

- Do not login to important accounts with a public computer (at the library or hotel lobby for example) or on a computer you do not own or control.

- It's a good habit to change your passwords regularly.

- Manage and encrypt your passwords with password management software.

- Do not let your browsers (FireFox, Chrome, Opera, IE, Safari) or FTP client programs save your passwords. Any password saved in the browser can be revealed with a simple click using the proper software script.

- Use secure connections when logging into accounts. Look for HTTPS in the browser address bar. Do not login to important accounts with HTTP or FTP connections, because the username and password in the message of a HTTP or FTP connection is unencrypted, and can be captured easily with a network protocol analyzer. That means that the password can be read or hacked with very little effort. Use HTTPS or SFTP connections instead.

Chapter 7

Summary

- Hackers don't guess. They use computers to try every combination until they get in to your account, or give up.

- Hackers are becoming ever more sophisticated with their password cracking software, so no password can ever be 100% safe. Our job is to minimize the risk by choosing and using longer and stronger passwords to make their job as hard as possible.

- Use a password manager to generate strong(er) passwords and to remember/manage them for you so you don't have to remember them all yourself!

- If you're not using a password manager, at least use longer passwords with substitution to increase the difficulty of cracking your password.

- Reusing passwords is asking for trouble. Having ANY accounts on the internet is like parking "in a bad part of town." Lock your car doors (by using strong(er) passwords) so it's less likely that the contents will be stolen!

Chapter 8: I can't share that, it's confidential!

What is the mistake?

As a coach, you probably hear great feedback from your clients about the incredibly awesome results they are getting as a direct result of working with you. The mistake that coaches make is thinking that there is no way to ethically use that great client feedback in a way that will bring you even more clients. Fortunately that's not entirely true, and I'll be sharing a way to easily and ethically turn around that mistake.

Why This Is a Mistake

As a coach you likely have some kind of confidentiality clause as part of your coaching intake form and contract. As a result, you probably think that everything that goes on between you and your client would be covered under that confidentiality agreement. And that's likely true (within the limits of the law). What coaches don't realize is that there are several ways to step outside of that confidentiality agreement and actually share the fantastic results your coaching clients are achieving by working with you.

What are the consequences of making this mistake and how critical are they?

The consequences of making this mistake could be relatively minor when compared to the password mistakes discussed in the last chapter. However there are still significant consequences that come from making this mistake. Those consequences are harder to measure because they are really in the form of a lost opportunity and lost revenue. Quantifying how many additional clients you didn't have join your coaching program because you didn't have great testimonials is difficult. But consider how much additional revenue any one of you customers brings. While it could be as little as $100 at the low end. At the high end it could be that you missed out on your very best coaching client who not only paid you thousands of dollars directly for coaching them, but also brought you six additional high-end clients as a result of their referrals. I'm sure you wouldn't want to miss out on that!

Chapter 8

Why and when do people tend to make this mistake?

The reason coaches make this mistake is because they have been well trained, and as part of that training have been told that the contents of the coaching sessions and the other interactions with their clients are confidential. And from an ethical standpoint that is as it should be.

However, this assumption only applies to you identifying the client and their specific results, not the client actually sharing their own results with others!

What should they do instead?

So the way to fix this and step outside of the limitations of confidentiality is to explicitly ask your coaching clients to put together a testimonial of the results they have gotten from working with you! Let them know that you would like to use their testimonial to help attract more "perfect clients" like them.

When a client understands the purpose of the testimonial, and is the one choosing what to share knowing that it will be publically visible, they become the one choosing to step outside of the realm of coach-client confidentiality. They are likely to be so happy with the results they have gained from coaching with you that they will gladly support you in building your coaching business and helping more people like them.

There are several ways to create testimonials that you can use to promote your coaching business and gain more clients. Regardless of which one you use, be sure to use a release form that has been approved by your legal counsel. The release form should inform the client that their testimonial may be publically viewable, and may be used to help promote your coaching business.

You can gather testimonials from your clients in a written form. Simply ask them to fill out the testimonial form in which they share their "Win" and the results of working with you (and sign it under the release section!)

You could also ask them to make a video testimonial for you. You could either ask them to do it on their own, or set up a specific time and place to video it for them. Smart phones with video capability are a great way to capture this type of testimonial quickly and easily. Remember to hold the smart phone horizontal so the video is wider than it is tall!

Another way would be to use a smart phone as a voice recorder to capture their testimonial. Or they could even leave their testimonial as a voicemail if you have a way to copy it off of your voicemail system that is!

You can increase the power of a written or audio testimonial by including a photo of your client along with the written words or audio. Be sure to ask them for a head shot, or take one with your smart phone, with their permission of course.

And just to be sure that your client is fully cognizant of how the testimonial is being used on your website, you could give them a printed copy of the testimonial page showing their glowing testimonial on it.

Oh, and be sure to let them know that they can share the link to your testimonial page so their friends can see it too. They may be excited with their new "celebrity status" on the internet and want to share it!

What should you do if you've already made this mistake? How do you fix it?

If you aren't currently asking your coaching clients for testimonials, then start. There is really no in-between position. You may not want to ask every single client for a testimonial. Some clients simply may not be a good fit for creating the kind of testimonial you want in order to attract your ideal client. Other clients will be able to provide you with a great testimonial that will attract your perfect client, and those are the ones you want to be sure to ask this week.

How do we prevent making this mistake moving forward?

It's unlikely that you'll make that mistake again, now that you know how to get around it. There is still some work that needs to be done in creating the Client Testimonial Release Form and having your legal counsel review it for you.

Any tools or insight to help people get results faster, easier, more efficiently?

Effective presentation of testimonials for use in promoting your coaching business will include these basic features in addition to the testimonial itself.

- Client name (Full name or first name plus initial)

- Location (City & State, especially if you think your business may ever draw clients from beyond your local area.)

- Job title (If appropriate)

- Client Photo (Putting a face on the testimonial increases trust that it's a real testimonial.)

One way to create great testimonial content is to coach the client to share in a "Before, During, After" format. What was the client's situation before working with you? What did your client experience during the process of coaching with you? What were the ultimate benefits and outcome of coaching with you?

Here is an example testimonial showing the Before, During, After format:

"Before I started coaching with Mary, I felt like I was fumbling around in the dark trying to find my life purpose and I felt like I didn't have a good reason to get up in the morning. My job left me feeling empty and drained. I really lacked direction in my life.

Once I started coaching with her, and we started working through her 12 step life purpose discovery process, I was amazed at the depth of feeling and passion that I found for my newly discovered life purpose. I have to laugh, because It had always been there, staring me in the face, but I just couldn't see it, or feel it, until Mary guided me through uncovering it.

Now that I have completed this coaching process with her, I'm thrilled by the amount of passion and drive I feel - not only to pursue my purpose in life, but also in the new job I started with a great company that pays me very well, and is in alignment with my newly rediscovered goals and values. They even help support me in my volunteer work as part of their community outreach program. I know I wouldn't be enjoying my life this way if I hadn't started coaching with Mary!"

Jane Smith
IT Department
Seattle, WA

What is one BIG piece of advice or "The Key" to avoiding this mistake in the future?

Start gathering testimonials to help promote your business, and help more clients today by making a list of the clients who expressed excitement from the breakthrough results they achieved from your coaching. Next contact them each individually, or talk with them at the end of their next coaching session, and ask if they would be willing to share a testimonial about their results from coaching with you. Discuss the written, audio, and video options for creating their testimonial and ask which they would prefer. Walk them through the Before, During, After testimonial format, and provide them with the testimonial and release form so they can get started creating their testimonial immediately.

Once you have a few testimonials, start using them to promote your coaching business, and be sure to add them to a "Client Results & Testimonials" page on your websites. You can even start creating this page before you have any testimonials, by adding your words about the results you have seen your clients achieve. By removing all personally identifiable information, you can start sharing some of the results your clients have gotten. While these are not as powerful as customer written testimonials, they are a good starting point for letting prospective clients know what kind of results are achievable through working with you.

Summary

- You can't share your clients' confidential coaching details, but your clients may when they create a testimonial of their wins and breakthroughs from coaching with you.

- Ask your clients if they would provide you with a testimonial that you could use to help promote your coaching business and help even more clients like them.

- While text testimonials are most common, audio, and video testimonials can have an even greater impact when provided by the right coaching client.

- Be sure to include the name and a photo of the client on your website (with their approval.)

- Suggest to the client that they use the before, during, after format for their testimonial.

- Be sure to get a signed testimonial release form that is approved by your legal counsel from your client, along with their testimonial.

Chapter 9: I'm busy! Besides, it really doesn't matter because they'll just read about it anyway

What is the mistake?

Thinking that the quality of your content is more important than how it looks can be very detrimental to your success. Not only will a poor or confusing website layout drive away potential customers, but so will bad graphics and lousy videos.

Why is it a mistake?

A new visitor will make a snap decision about your website in the first few seconds of their visit. They either decide they don't like it and leave, or they decide they like it enough to hang around a bit longer and continue exploring it. And that is all done before they start to read or consume any of your content!

What are the consequences of making this mistake and how critical are they?

If your site looks amateurish then visitors are much more likely to leave than stick around. Visitors consider the graphics, colors, overall layout, the fonts used, and even whether or not the menu names provide an instant understanding for navigation around your site. New visitors are looking for something they can connect with in a positive way and are quick to judge your site, and you, by their very first impression of your site. When they are searching on your site for specific information, and are trying to find it quickly, they are more apt to quickly "cross you off the list" than they are to hang around and dig for the information they are seeking.

Why and when do people tend to make this mistake?

Let's face it. We are all very busy these days. Not only are we creating our websites and content, but the rest of our marketing material as well. Ideal client avatars, mission statements, and signature speeches all need to be researched and created. There comes a point where "done" trumps "good" simply so that we can get on to the next task on our long list of "necessary" items as we start building our coaching practice. This is a dangerous time when asking for outside help is vital to our success because we are so busy and may lose sight of what is truly important to our ultimate success.

What should they do instead?

There are several levels of "asking for help with your website." Feedback from people you trust to "say it like it is" without sugar-coating it is vital. There are times when we fall in love with an idea or concept that should have been abandoned long ago, but without external feedback we may never see that.

That was exactly the case for me with the cover design for this book. I spent all day one Sunday creating what I thought was a really cool book cover layout. When I asked some of my friends, and especially those who are much closer to my ideal client, for feedback on it, it was not positive... but it was very helpful! As a result, I hired a cover designer to create the cover you see today.

There are some website jobs or tasks that are simply not worth struggling with, graphics for example. If you're not a graphic designer, or don't have killer skills with graphic tools like PhotoShop, you are much better off to outsource the creation of the graphics for your website...and free reports...and videos. Not only will it take much less of your personal time, but the results are likely to be much better too.

Header graphics for your website, 3D cover images for the free report you use as your opt-in "bribe," and the graphics used with your blog posts are all examples of things you can outsource to someone with "mad skills" and save yourself the time and the headache of creating them yourself.

What should you do if you've already made this mistake? How do you fix it?

Even if you've already gone down the road of creating these graphical resources yourself, it would be advisable to get feedback from that "blunt" friend or colleague.

If you're still faced with creating those graphical elements and looking for resources, then look into sites like Presenter Media, iStock photo, and Fiverr. Those sites in particular will give you a variety of options for inspiration as well as outsourced workers who are ready, willing, and able to help create your custom graphics just the way you want them.

I have arranged for a special offer from PresenterMedia, iStockPhoto, and VideoBlocks for my readers to help you get started with your website and marketing graphics. You can learn more about them by visiting: `http://CoachesMarketingToolbox.com/media`. All of the media related resources and special offers can be found on this page.

Chapter 9

How do we prevent making this mistake moving forward?

The first step to preventing this mistake moving forward is to be aware that it is a mistake as well as a trap that is very easy to fall into because of your busy schedule.

The second step is to actually outsource the creation of some graphics. Fiverr is a great place to start becoming familiar with the graphic outsourcing process because with "gigs" starting at $5, so you really aren't risking much even if it goes horribly wrong.

The third step is to catch yourself when you are going down the path to creating something that A) is not your brilliance, and/or B) will realistically take longer to do yourself than it would to outsource it. (And don't forget to consider the cost in lost revenue because you're working on graphics, rather than coaching a paying client!) Heck, the gigs are only $5, so buy three from different people and choose the one you like the best! It's only five bucks you're risking after all!

Any tools or insight to help people get results faster, easier, more efficiently?

When searching Fiverr for "the right" person, be sure to sort by Highest Rating, and then not only look at their example work portfolio, but read the reviews.

With many of the Fiverr providers, you can "add a $5 tip" and are likely to get extra, faster, or better service as a result.

If you're not sure if someone can create the graphics you're interested in, be sure to message them ahead of buying a gig from them and discuss what you want. They will be able to advise you if they are the one to go with, or not, before you invest any more time with them.

The more information you can provide to a graphic designer the better, especially if you have something specific in mind. Including example graphics (or URLs to them) or even stick figure drawings that you created in PowerPoint or Paint can help. Maybe you're better with paper and pencil. Include a photo of it from your smart phone. Write it up as a document with pictures & URLS and send them the DOC file or save it as a PDF and send that. I've had great luck getting exactly what I want with this approach.

On the other hand, you can also "give them free license" with just a few suggestions, or comments on how you will be using the graphic, and maybe some information about you and your business to give them the "flavor" of what you're looking for.

What is one BIG piece of advice or "The Key" to avoiding this mistake in the future?

The best advice I can share about this mistake is to realize that investing the extra time, effort, and money to create a professional looking result will pay off in the long run. Potential clients will see you as having a professional business even if you're just getting started! If you're like most people, you would prefer to work with someone who gives a professional appearance, rather than someone who oozes their "amateur" status.

Here is a bonus tidbit to consider regarding another form of "graphic" – Videos. Studies have shown that 60% of the "perceived quality" of a video is judged subjectively by the quality of the audio! Make sure the audio on your videos is good. Background noise, room echo, the audio being too loud or too quiet, background music, etc. all affect the perceived audio quality. Many of these factors are much easier to "fix" by using the right equipment and environment up front, rather than in post-production after the video is shot. Fiverr may offer gigs that can help fix this sort of thing after the video is shot, so take a look

Summary:

- You only get one "First Impression." Make it count by having quality, professional looking marketing material, including your website, graphics, and videos.

- If you don't already have "mad graphic skills" don't create your own graphics. Outsource the job to someone who does, and focus on your areas of brilliance instead. You want to be hired for your expertise and skill, so be sure to hire others for theirs.

- Communicating your graphic ideas to someone else can be challenging. Use examples, and include URLs to graphics you like (or don't like) along with words to describe what you want. Include information about you, your business, your brand, and how you're going to use the graphic to help the designer to get the flavor of what you want, and you'll have a better result.

They say a picture says a thousand words. Don't let your graphics say the wrong words!

Chapter 10: I don't want to annoy people. They'll call me when they are ready.

What is the mistake?

As a new coach you are likely to be very enthusiastic about the value of coaching and have shared your enthusiasm with lots of people and potential clients. You may also feel like you don't want to continue to bug them by contacting them over and over again and asking them to become a coaching client. You probably felt that would be pushy and you don't want to be "one of those people."

You probably thought that since you have talked with them, and given them your card, that they would call you when they are ready for coaching.

The reality is that most likely they will never contact you, and may have even forgotten you are a coach. As brutal as that sounds, it's probably highly likely because you didn't do one critical thing: entice them to join your mailing list so you can continue to market to them in a professional manner.

The idea of regularly sending emails out to potential clients may have triggered a response in you like, "I don't want to annoy people. They'll call me when they are ready."

Why This Is a Mistake

This mistake is very dangerous to the health of your business, and especially your new coaching business. As you probably recognize, you constantly need to be on the lookout for, and recruiting, new coaching clients for your business. Even if you have a "full" coaching practice right now, eventually someone will complete their cycle and move on, leaving you with a hole to fill with a new client.

What are the consequences of making this mistake and how critical are they?

If you had a mailing list of potential clients who have raised their hand and said they are interested in knowing more about how you could help them through your coaching, wouldn't you think it would be relatively easy to find a new client to re-fill your coaching practice? On the other hand, if you don't have a list of prospective coaching clients at your fingertips, how long will it take, and how much effort are you going to have to apply, in order to fill that hole with a new paying client?

The other consequence of making this mistake is that it results in you not being "top of mind" when your potential client is ready to take the next step and explore what coaching with you can do for them. Maybe they met you...once...six months ago...and haven't heard from you since. Do you really think they are going to remember the coaching services you have to offer...or have any idea where your business card is?

Why and when do people tend to make this mistake?

Coaches make this mistake for a couple of reasons. First is the obvious one about not wanting to "drive away potential clients" by constantly hounding them to join you for coaching. While this IS a valid concern on one hand, there is still a piece missing from this puzzle that will change your whole understanding of this overall picture.

What should they do instead?

The solution to this dilemma of how to stay in front of your potential coaching clients, without constantly "pestering" them, is actually quite simple. Provide them ongoing value on a for free, and deliver it right to their email Inbox on a regular basis.

Let me walk you through the whole process. Let's assume you meet someone in line at the local

Starbucks coffee house, and strike up a conversation because they look like someone who might be your ideal client. During the course of the conversation you give them one of your business cards and ask them to, "Give me a call when you're ready to learn more about how I can help you through coaching." You may never see that person again, and your business card is likely to be either buried somewhere or just end up in the recycling bin. That's a pretty normal outcome for this type of scenario.

However, let's add one small, but critical detail. When you hand them your business card, you tell them that on the back of that card is a link to a free report (about some topic that your ideal client would be VERY interested in knowing about) and they can download it for free simply by visiting that website page and signing up. Or, you might tell them that you have a free, three part "mini-video-course" they could sign up for that would walk them through (some topic that your ideal client would be VERY interested in knowing) and you'd love to send it to them when they sign up.

How much more likely do you think that person would be to take action as a result of this second scenario than the first? If what you are offering them for free (in exchange for their email address and permission to send them more great tips, tricks, and resources over time) is of any significant interest to them, they are likely to sign up. And once they do, you will have a way to contact that prospective coaching client virtually forever, or at least until they unsubscribe from your list.

There are a few key things to remember. The "opt-in bribe" has to be so juicy sounding and valuable that they feel like they MUST HAVE IT! That's where crafting a great offer becomes key. And remember, the ONLY thing you are "selling" at this point is getting them to join your list in exchange for the juicy opt-in gift that you are giving them. Don't try to "sell" them anything more than that! Moving them closer to becoming your client is the purpose of subsequent messages delivered over time.

The next key thing to remember is that you will want to have your email autoresponder all set up to not only immediately send them that juicy opt-in bribe, but also regular messages for the next week to ten days.

The final key action to take is to continue sending some juicy content to the people on your list, every week to two weeks, or every month at the very least. You want them to remember you, and not think, "Who is this email from? I don't remember them!" The only way you can guarantee that is by sending great content regularly.

Now there is one thing that I want to go back and expand upon. When you set up your autoresponder to deliver that juicy opt-in bribe, you will also want to set up automatic delivery of a fat handful of other great content at the same time. It is critical that over the first 7-10 days you establish and build a relationship with them. Send them great content those first few days, and introduce yourself, while sharing content that is relevant to them. By doing that, not only are you establishing what they can expect from the relationship (that you will be giving them great stuff regularly) but you will also be building the "Know-Like-Trust" factor with them. And that KLT factor is critical to your continued success in getting them to not only remember who you are and what you have to offer, but also continuing to open and read your email messages when they arrive.

The higher the KLT factor, the more likely they are to pay attention to you, share your messages with others (thus spreading your reach and influence) and think of YOU when they are ready to take the next step to hiring a coach.

What should you do if you've already made this mistake? How do you fix it?

If you have already made this mistake and neglected to build a relationship with your list, then I have a suggestion. Once you have created your opt-in follow up sequence and added it to your autoresponder, go ahead and send out those messages to your "old list members." You may actually want to segregate your "old list members" from your "new list members." Create a new list in your autoresponder dashboard and change your opt-in offer to point to the new list so they will receive the new KLT building messages. You can then manually send out the KLT messages to your old list. You may get a bunch of unsubscribes when you do that, but those are probably people who were not paying any attention to you in the first place. It is very common to get unsubscribes every time you mail your list, and that's a good thing. By unsubscribing they are telling you they aren't interested, so they don't belong on your list of prospective customers anyway!

How do we prevent making this mistake moving forward?

By now you probably see quite clearly why not building an email list and having an autoresponder deliver great, relevant content is such a big mistake and can be deadly to the rapid growth of your coaching business and income!

While it's unlikely you'll make this mistake again, or at least it is once you've put all of the pieces in place, there is still some investment required to make all of this happen.

Any tools or insight to help people get results faster, easier, more efficiently?

There are at least five major pieces that you will need in order to build your list and start adding prospective clients to it.

- An Email Autoresponder Service

- An Opt-In page (commonly referred to as a "squeeze page")

- A Juicy Opt-In bribe (to help "squeeze" their email address out of them)

- An Autoresponder Email Sequence that delivers your initial juicy content and builds KLT

- Additional Juicy Content that you can send to your list after the initial "welcome" sequence.

For my autoresponder I use Aweber. I've been very happy with them over the years. They have a multi-tiered pricing structure that should work very well for coaches. Their base level (at the time that I'm writing this) is up to 500 subscribers and an unlimited number of Emails sent each month. As a coach, especially in the beginning, it's unlikely that you will need more. But if you do, the price increases are reasonable for each additional subscriber tier. They have years of experience working to keep the deliverability of your emails high. In addition to being able to broadcast emails to your subscribers, you can create and send schedule sequences of emails to be delivered automatically through their autoresponder features.

One of my personal friends and marketing mentor, Jim Edwards, has created some online Wizards that can really help you when it comes to creating your squeeze page, opt-in bribe, and autoresponder email message sequence. I've been a member of his Easy Online Wizards since it was launched, and have found it not only invaluable to me, but the number of hours it has saved me in creating each of those from scratch is substantial.

I have arranged for a special offer from Aweber and also Jim Edwards for access to his Easy Online Wizards just for my readers. You can learn more about them by visiting: `http://CoachesMarketingToolbox.com/lists`. Both the Aweber special offer and the Easy Online Wizards offer are there. (Rumor has it that Jim may have talked me into adding some other bonuses there too!)

What is one BIG piece of advice or "The Key" to avoiding this mistake in the future?

My best advice for you now is to invest in your business growth and sustainability by planning and implementing the powerful strategies outlined here. By doing so you will be taking a very powerful step toward sustainability and growth of your business and client base. Without this type of marketing strategy, your path to business and coaching success will be a much more challenging one.

So get started today by examining, "What is it that you could offer your prospective ideal client that would really grab their attention and compel them to join your list?" Once you've answered that question, you're well on the road to successful implementation of this business building strategy.

Summary

- Having a way to contact your prospective ideal clients is critical to growing your business and income, and maintaining a full, thriving, coaching practice.

- Offering a juicy opt-in bribe is the best way to get their email address so you can continue to contact your coaching prospects by email.

- The best way to stay in touch (and top of mind) with your prospective ideal clients is through having regular "juicy content" email messages delivered to your list. These can be both as pre-programmed autoresponder messages and individual broadcast messages when you have something new or special to share with them...like a new opening to work with you!

- It is crucial to contact your new list members very frequently in the first two weeks or so, in order to establish a pattern in their mind of delivering great value to them on a regular basis, as well as building the Know-Like-Trust factor.

- The easiest way to get started creating and implementing this vital business building tool is using the recommended tools and resources. Figuring out how to do all of that on your own is not only frustrating, but likely to leave you with less than optimal results. Follow the fast path to success and use the recommended tools instead. Don't "reinvent the wheel" – let the wizards guide you through easily assembling what you need with proven components instead.

Chapter 11: If they are interested they will know what to do. There is no need to manipulate them

What is the mistake?

As a new coach you probably don't have very much experience creating marketing material. As a result you may feel like you are manipulating your audience when you give them a call to action. Some new coaches are so averse to using a call to action that they have trouble even asking their prospects to go watch one of their YouTube videos in which they share great content and then ask the viewer to schedule a Strategy-Action-Discovery session with them.

Why is it a mistake?

This is actually a very big mistake. What most coaches who are new to marketing don't realize is that using a call to action can massively increase their results, particularly when it is a very specific call to action. As a coach you are likely focused on empowering your clients and helping to guide them to the results they want to achieve. So you may think they will feel manipulated when you use a call to action that tells them what to do.

What are the consequences of making this mistake and how critical are they?

People are actively looking for the next step, and by not telling them what to do next, through a call to action, you are actually doing them a disservice. Without a call to action they have to stop and take the time to figure out what to do next. With as busy as we all are these days, and with so many things calling for our attention, they may simply get distracted before they figure out how to take the next step with you.

Have you ever enjoyed a particular YouTube video, for example, and wanted to know how to learn more from that person, but you couldn't figure out how? It's likely that you invested a second or two looking around the page and then you got caught up in the "related videos" thumbnails. You probably never did take any more action with that person, now did you? Without an explicit call to action telling you what to do next to engage further with that person, you simply wandered off somewhere else.

By not having a call to action in their video, something as simple as,

"If you liked what you saw here, be sure to visit my website where I have lots more cool stuff like this available for you. Visit www.MyWebsite.com now!"

they (and YOU!) totally missed out on sharing the great information that is on their website.

Why and when do people tend to make this mistake?

We have all been subjected to the pushy "used car" style salesman who is constantly, and loudly, trying to get you to "BUY! BUY! BUY!" and we hate that feeling ourselves. As a coach you want to make sure that you don't come across that way to your prospective clients, so you may almost go overboard the other way by not giving them a call to action.

As a coach, rather than a marketing expert, you may also have a misunderstanding about what is a call to action? A call to action, or CTA, is considered anything you say or do that indicate the next step that you want someone to take.

You are in business to make money by helping people through coaching. (If that wasn't the case, then why are you charging clients?) So logically, the next step you want them to take is some action that leads them closer your goals – gaining more money by helping more clients. And there is nothing wrong with that because you both benefit from the coaching relationship!

What should they do instead?

It's easy to start with simple a CTA such as "Find this post useful? Then LIKE it!" or "Want more? Visit my blog at http://www.MyBlog.com" or even "Click here to sign up for a free Strategy-Action-Discovery session!"

As strange as it may sound, part of the purpose of doing this consistently is to train them to click on the links in your emails because you have ensured those links always lead to great stuff! This is especially true when it comes to Emails that you send to your prospective clients through your autoresponder. That way they will be looking forward to clicking on the links in your emails and benefitting from what else it is that you have to share with them.

What should you do if you've already made this mistake? How do you fix it?

While you may not be able to easily change things you've created in the past, you can start adding Calls To Action in every communication you send out starting today. Start with your email signature block and add a CTA that leads to your blog. Then take the next step and include CTAs in your social media posts and messages. Whichever approach you choose to use, get started using CTAs today!

How do we prevent making this mistake moving forward?

In the beginning, it may feel funny to use Calls To Action, but over time it will become a natural part of the way you do business. Taking that first step and getting started by using CTAs is how you prevent making that mistake moving forward.

Any tools or insight to help people get results faster, easier, more efficiently?

Take a few moments to make a list of CTAs that apply to your business so that later you don't have to stop and think about what to write. By having a pre-written list of CTAs you may find one that fits perfectly and you can simply cut and paste it. Or you will see one that inspires you to write the perfect CTA for inclusion right now.

My good friend and marketing mentor, Jim Edwards, has a "Stealth Close" wizard that Creates "Under-The-Radar" Calls To Action that you can use in all of your marketing material. It's one of Jim's Easy Online Wizards that I use regularly in my business.

I have arranged for a special offer from Jim Edwards for access to his Easy Online Wizards just for my readers. You can learn more about this special offer and the wizards by visiting: **http://CoachesMarketingToolbox.com/cta**. (Rumor has it that Jim may have talked me into adding some other bonuses there too!)

What is one BIG piece of advice or "The Key" to avoiding this mistake in the future?

The key take-away from this is to include some kind of CTA in EVERYTHING that you do. Include a CTA in your email signature. It could be for a free Strategy-Action-Discovery Session, or a free report on three quick and easy things that can help <description of your ideal customer> get <some benefit or result they want.> At a minimum, it should say "Visit my website at http://www. MyWebsite.com."

When you post something on Facebook that is business related use a CTA at the end of the post. Tell them to LIKE the post, and visit http://www.MyWebsite.com for more.

Get into the habit of thinking, "What action do I want someone who sees this to take as their very next step?" and then add that as a CTA.

Summary:

- Calls To Action are beneficial to you and your potential client. They help guide them to the next step on the path to benefitting from what you have to share with them.

- CTAs should be included in everything you do (that is business related) so the reader/watcher/listener knows what to do next and won't get distracted before they figure it out themselves.

- You can start using CTAs today simply by adding one to your Email signature block...and your very next blog post...and Facebook post.

- CTAs don't turn you into a slimy used car salesman. They guide the person to the next action from which THEY can receive benefit on the path to working with you more closely as a coach.

Chapter 12: The Internet never goes down, besides my site is too small to hack!

What is the mistake?

Not making backups is a mistake which can be deadly to your website, your income, and your business.

When most people think of backups, they think of backing up their computer in case of a disk failure, or corruption, or as a (partial) recovery plan if their laptop is stolen. The problem is that while it's great (and VITAL) to have backups of your computer, the loss of the content of your website can be even more devastating. This is especially true if you sell any products, or have a membership area as part of your website. When your website "goes away" so do the sales and your income from the products you sell there. Plus your customers are going to be upset because they can't access the members' area!

Why This Is a Mistake

Earlier today, a friend of mine posted on Facebook that her computer had to be sent back to the manufacturer after the disk crashed. She wrote that she had lost two days of work...or so she thought! Once she started looking into it, she had lost a LOT more than just those two days of work.

So now not only has she lost her data, but she's without her computer for days and days until it returns from the manufacturer. Plus, there is no guarantee that the computer manufacturer will be able to recover the data.

She went on to say that if she had to send the disk drive back to the disk manufacturer for data recovery, it would cost $1500 and even then there was no guarantee that they would be able to recover the data either. She got quite a lesson in the cost of not having a backup for the data on her business computer.

She's paying – big time! – for not having backups of the data on her computer. Faced today with the prospect of having to recreate everything she lost, I'm sure she would happily go back in time and pay a few thousand dollars for a solid, reliable backup solution instead.

It's also definitely a mistake, and potentially an even bigger one, to not back up your website too.

If your website gets hacked, ALL of your data, and the comments on your blog posts, and the videos, and PDF's, etc. could all be unrecoverably gone!

Sure, you may have the documents, and videos, and PDFs with the original content that you used to create for your website initially, but now you have to go through all of the work to completely wipe out your WordPress install, and databases, and delete all the directories, just to make sure there isn't any malicious code left anywhere.

Then you have to reinstall WordPress, and your theme, and plugins, and customize your setup, and upload your graphics, and videos, and pdfs, and THEN you can start reconfiguring the content of your website based on the copies of the original documents that you had.

You did keep copies of your design notes and every blog post, edit, and piece of content didn't you? How long do you think it would take to recreate your website from scratch? What would that cost you in time, effort, money, AND sanity?

But your web host has backups of your website, don't they? Do they? How old are the backups? And will they be willing or able to help you recover your COMPLETE website? How long would it take, and how much would it cost? If you rely on your web hosting company to provide the backups, it's like sending a clear plastic bag through the mail system with $10,000.00 in cash in it and counting on it getting to its assigned destination intact. Sure, the mail system workers are probably very honest, but are you really willing to risk your business on that hope?

A couple of days ago, I went to visit a friend's website and I saw that it had been hacked. As far as I can tell, he lost everything that was there. It wasn't some big, prominent website that was begging to be a prize in some hacker's trophy case. On top of that, when I checked again today, the problem is still there. I don't think he even knows about it yet! (Yes, I did send him an email letting him know.) Do you check your website every day to see what your customers would find there?

As part of the security measures I have installed and configured on my website, I have a plugin that will block someone who tries to repeatedly login using the wrong credentials. Whenever they get to 16 wrong attempts, I automatically get an email. I've been getting a bunch of those recently from one of my sites. The good news is that that particular IP address is locked out for 24 hours. The bad news is that someone is actively trying to hack their way into my website. Fortunately, I have a good solid backup of the site. Should the worst happen, I know I will be able to recover quickly.

What are the consequences of making this mistake and how critical are they?

As you read in the stories of what happened to my friends, the consequences of making this mistake can be devastating and extremely difficult to recover from. Sometimes it is simply impossible to recover all of your data.

At the end of this chapter, I'll be sharing the consequences of the mistake I made by not having timely backups of my data a few years ago. It broke my spirit with respect to that particular project, and I've never been able to fully engage with it ever since. The lost revenue alone from that "intangible" aspect is well into the thousands if not tens of thousands of dollars.

Why and when do people tend to make this mistake?

There are four primary reasons that people make this critical mistake and don't have backups when they urgently need them.

First, they "never get around to it." I'm not implying that they are lazy, but rather that there appear to be some "higher priority tasks" that are "more urgent" than putting in place a regular backup solution.

Second, they don't know how, and haven't invested sufficient time, effort, and money to find a solution.

Third, they are relying on "someone else" to backup THEIR data for them and haven't investigated the truth of that assumption.

The fourth reason could either be considered misguided arrogance, or misguided "hope" because they are either hoping that they won't ever have a problem, or believe that they are "too insignificant" in the larger scheme of the Internet to show up on some hacker's radar as a target.

Unfortunately, any one of these reasons can land you in the same place – dead in the water with no way to easily recover from the problem.

What should they do instead?

The solution, or fix for this problem can be relatively simple, but you have to actually implement it. The solution is to put in place a backup strategy and then actually follow through and use it!

There are several things to consider, especially when it comes to human nature. Backups are unlikely to get done if it requires human intervention every time. So for example promising yourself that you WILL do a manual backup daily is highly likely to be doomed to failure on an ongoing basis. Hit and miss is the best you are likely to achieve and the amount of time between hits is likely to increase over time!

So putting in place an automatic backup strategy is much more likely to be successful than relying on ourselves to not be overwhelmed by our task list, and remember to do daily backups...along with running the rest of our business!

Another thing to consider is how much we are willing to risk when it comes to backups. There are two classes of backup, on-site, and off-site. In many ways off-site backups are better because if there is a localized disaster, like a fire, flood, earthquake, electrical surge, or weather event, then your backup data is not in the same physical location and is thus are more likely to remain available for restoration.

There are internet based services which you can subscribe to that can provide daily (or more likely nightly) backups of the data on your computer(s) for a monthly fee. Remember to weigh their monthly membership cost against the complete loss of your data, and what it would take to recover from a catastrophic total loss event, rather than just dollars and cents. Consider it like an insurance policy for your computer data. It's just another cost of being in business.

The availability of network drives which can be configured for redundant data storage is another option for on-site backups. Many of these devices come with automatic backup software that can be used to create scheduled backups of every computer on your network. They can also be used as a repository for archives of (older) data that you don't need to access quickly on a daily basis. Personally, I have a number of video training packages that I store on my network drive. I seldom need to access them, and because they are video, the take up a lot of disk space – much more than I want to have tied up on my laptop for example. Whenever I need to reference them, I can simply do so by connecting to my business network and access is immediately available.

This type of daily backup strategy is great, but it could leave one "exposed" to data loss between backups. Fortunately, there are several strategies for dealing with that as well.

One of my personal favorites is DropBox. What I generally (try to remember to do – hey, I'm human!) is to save whatever it is that I'm working on in a subfolder of the DropBox folder on my computer. That way, every time the DOC, or XLS, or PPT, or PDF, or MP4, or MP3, or anything other file I'm working on is saved (including autosaves for instance) it is automatically uploaded to "the cloud" where my DropBox account lives. Thus there is a local copy on my computer's disk drive, and another copy in my DropBox account in the cloud. My exposure to loss of these files has been minimized down to the time between saves or auto-saves, plus whatever time it takes to upload to the cloud across my internet connection. With typical auto save settings, that can be on the order of five minutes.

Another cool advantage of DropBox is that your files are automatically synchronized across multiple computers. Each computer (Mac & PC) which has DropBox loaded on it will have an identical copy of the files stored in the cloud. That way you can be working on your desktop computer in your office, and take your laptop to the coffee shop and seamlessly keep your files synchronized thorough DropBox...at least if you are logged into the internet at the coffee shop. And if not, then the synchronization will occur with the next time you are connected to the internet.

One other thing about DropBox – there are Apps for Apple mobile devices (iPad, iPhone, iTouch) as well as Android devices, so you can access your DropBox data on your mobile device. The mobile Apps allow you to select how much data is loaded onto the device itself. That way you don't overwhelm your mobile device's storage with files you don't really need. You can also explicitly load files onto the mobile device for access while you are "off network" such as when the mobile device is in Airplane Mode. I've used that capability to pre-load training videos I wanted to watch during cross-country flights, and it has worked marvelously! (And it's much easier than having to connect and upload the video files through iTunes!)

It's great to have your computers backed up, but what about your website? There are still a number of options, but they are less commonly visible to most people.

My personal favorite website backup strategy is WPtwin software. It allows me to completely clone a website – pages, posts, comments, videos, audios, PDFs, and any other files in the directories – so that I have a fast and easy way to recover from website hacks, or human mistakes that result in data loss.

There are two "flavors" of WPTwin, the manual clone method, and the scheduled, automatic clone method. If you only update your website once or twice a week for instance, you could probably get away with the manual method with minimal risk. (You would risk losing any blog comments that came in after the last clone/backup.) However if your website is an active one with a blog that gets lots of traffic and comments, you probably want to consider adding the automatic clone method and relatively frequent (daily or more) clone/backups.

WPtwin can also be used to quickly and easily move your website from one hosting company to another as your business grows and your website needs more "hosting horsepower." That's also the same process that is used to recover from having your site hacked.

If your site has been hacked, and if you have a current backup (the one prior to the hacking) you can probably recover very quickly – often in well under an hour. What I recommend is starting the recovery process by cloning the hacked site, and carefully labeling the file as the hacked version, while being very careful NOT to overwrite your good backups. (Having access to this clone can be very useful in figuring out how you got hacked so you can plug the hole!)

Then I would completely uninstall and erase your entire Wordpress website, and Wordpress databases. (Your hosting company can probably help you with this as necessary. You want to be sure you don't erase the wrong stuff!) Once you are back to an "empty" state, you can start building back up with a fresh install of WordPress. Once WordPress is installed and activated, you can use WPtwin to deploy the cloned content back onto your website. Once that is completed, your website should be back up and running as if nothing had ever happened.

There are other WordPress backup methods, strategies, and plugins. Be sure to do your research and understand what it takes to re-deploy the backup if you need it. Some of the backup methods I've seen appear to be easy to create the backups but turn out to be very difficult to deploy when you need to restore your site.

With whatever website backup method you choose, be sure to test it out so that you KNOW that the backup strategy worked and that you can redeploy it with what you consider to be a reasonable level of effort.

What should you do if you've already made this mistake? How do you fix it?

If you don't have any kind of backup solution in place right now, your website and computer data are living on borrowed time. Invest the time and money in finding the right solution for you, right now, so you can start sleeping better at night knowing that you have a way to recover from catastrophic circumstances. If the stores of my friend's losses haven't convinced you yet, be sure to read about my data loss at the end of this chapter. Having defeat stolen out of the jaws of victory like that is devastating. Don't let that happen to you!

How do we prevent making this mistake moving forward?

The best use for a backup is to never ever need it. You can move closer to that scenario by using good security measures on both your computers and websites. This would include strong passwords, and virus protection for your computers, and appropriate security measures for your website including security plugins and strong passwords.

Any tools or insight to help people get results faster, easier, more efficiently?

DropBox is a tool that I have connected to all of my computers and mobile devices. As a result, I can easily share files and folders between my computers and mobile devices. I find it much easier to use DropBox to transfer a video file that I want to access a few times on my iPhone or iPad than it is it do so through iTunes. In addition, by placing the file in my DropBox folder, it is automatically copied to my secure folder on DropBox.com, as well as each of my computers and mobile devices which are connected to the internet and logged in to DropBox.

DropBox has a special offer program that can help get you additional space for free. I've included the details on how to sign up for dropbox and get extra space all for free over at: `http://CoachesMarketingToolbox.com/backup`.

WPtwin is definitely my favorite website backup and cloning tool. I use it to backup each of my websites whenever I make a change to it. I also have the upgraded version which allows me to schedule automatic backup-clone creation on a regular basis. That way, if a hacker ever does wipe out my precious website, I have a quick and easy way to recover from it.

I recommend that you take a few moments to find out more about WPtwin and how easy it is to use by visiting: `http://CoachesMarketingToolbox.com/backup`. Using WPtwin to back up my websites is what allows me to sleep soundly at night, because I know that should a hacker compromise my site, that I can be up and running again very quickly, and without having to "diagnose" what they did to my site, and somehow undo it. I simply delete the old compromised site, and deploy the clone, and I'm up and running again in a few minutes.

There are a number of other computer backup solutions out there. Technology is always marching forward and it can be challenging to keep up with what is the best solution for you today. When you visit `http://CoachesMarketingToolbox.com/backup` you will also find my latest recommendations for hardware and software solutions for creating backups of your computer. Be sure that you have a good solution that works for you by starting your search there. I also have some other backup and security tips that I will share with you on that page.

What is one BIG piece of advice or "The Key" to avoiding this mistake in the future?

Make a commitment to yourself today to lower your risk of loss by determining the best backup strategy for your business, and then implement and use it! Your business data and website is too important to risk losing!

Summary

- The risks of not having and using a backup strategy are large, as are the costs to recover if you don't have access to a backup when you need it.

- You will need to determine for yourself whether on-site or off-site backups for your computer data are most appropriate for your business situation and risk tolerance level.

- Network drives configured for redundancy can provide a reasonable level of backup security as long as the scheduled backups actually occur. (The computer has to be On at the scheduled time for the backup to occur.)

- DropBox is a wonderful tool that can also act as a mini-backup for some of your files.

- WPtwin is the tool that I use myself for cloning (and backing up) my websites.

No one ever has a "minor need" for access to a backup. It is always a desperate need because something has gone horribly wrong. Don't wait until it's too late!

Before we "close the book" on these 12 mistakes, I wanted to share one more story about what can happen when you don't have a "constant backup" strategy. This tale strikes much closer to home, because it happened to me personally!

A couple of years ago, I too suffered from a disk crash and extremely painful data loss. At 2:00 AM I finished putting the finishing touches on a big project that I had been working on for months. I was THRILLED with how it had turned out, and exhausted at the same time, given the hour. So I made a fatal mistake. Instead of copying everything in the project over to my network drive as an immediate backup, I decided to do it in the morning.

The next morning, when I started the computer I was greeted with the message, "Operating System Not Found!" Those are four words that will just about stop your heart, or at least it nearly did mine!

So the rest of the story is that this was my big "video editing machine" which had all of my best and fastest hardware and software on it. Because of where the computer case is located, one of my cats used it as a "step" when jumping up and down onto the table. The afternoon before, I had watched (helplessly) as my cat had jumped down especially hard, and the computer case had banged into the table leg. I was a little bit worried at that moment, but everything appeared to be fine, and the computer continued to work for the rest of the day while I continued to work on that big project.

As it turned out, that bang into the table leg was hard enough to crash the disk head into the disk platter and literally peel the data off of the disk platter like a potato peeler takes the skin off of a potato! The data was still "inside the disk drive" but it had been rearranged into a fine dust spread around the inside of the disk drive case itself – never to be read again!

If I had been using a "constant" backup system, or even had been using my DropBox folders properly, I would have had a much easier path to recovery.

PLEASE don't make the mistake that I did! Create and keep your backups current!

Conclusion

Chapter Highlights & Summary

We've covered a lot of material in the last 12 chapters. By recognizing and understanding critical mistakes that can repel your ideal customers you will better be able to eliminate them from your website and marketing.

Chapter 12: The internet never goes down and besides, my site is too small for anyone to want to hack it.

Not making backups of the data on your computer and of your website may not seem like something that would repel your customers...on the surface. The problems come with the consequences of not making the backups. The cost to your coaching business in time, effort, AND money is not to be taken lightly. Computer crashes often leave very little if any of your information recoverable. Finding out that your website has been hacked gives you a sense of violation and loss that is unparalleled. Don't get caught this way. Create a backup plan for your data and website and then implement it! Implement it today. Back up your most vital information to an external drive, or even a USB thumb drive immediately. It may not seem like much by comparison to a full backup solution, but it will at least give you a fighting chance and a place to start rebuilding from if or when the worst should happen. You owe it to yourself, your business, your income, and your customers.

Chapter 11: If they are interested they know what to do. There is no need to manipulate them.

Calls to action are not manipulative. Your potential customers, your website visitors, and your clients are all waiting for you to tell them what to do as their next step. While they may or may not take that next step you suggest, without some kind of call to action they are much more likely to do nothing at all! Including a call to action is actually being of service to them because by the time they have read, or watched, or listened to the content you are sharing with them and have actually made it to the end, they are already engaged with you. If they were not interested in the topic and the information you are sharing they would have stopped paying attention and left already. By the time they get to the end of consuming that information, they are looking for you to tell them how to take the next step on this road they have been on. Give them a call to action that tells them what the next step is to take...and move them closer to working with you directly. You know you are providing value and service to them, so invite them in!

Chapter 10: I don't want to annoy people. They'll call me when they are ready.

Waiting for new clients to contact you "when they are ready" is not only a waste of time, but is a serious mistake that will keep you poor and your coaching practice empty. The best potential clients for any business are the ones who have raised their hand and said they're interested in knowing more. You can gather these people onto your email list by offering them an ethical bribe in exchange for their email address. That free report, or mini video course, along with delivering great relevant content on a frequent regular basis will not only keep your coaching prospects "warm" but will continue to build the know-like-trust factor that leads them to working with you more closely. Create your ethical bribe and setup an opt-in page that offers it on your website. Add that specific URL to your business card. Be sure to point out the invitation to join you every time you hand someone your business card.

Chapter 9: I'm busy! Besides, it really doesn't matter because they'll just read about it anyway.

Quality content is vital to having an effective website and marketing material in general. However it is a mistake to believe that the content is more important than the presentation. Having good graphics, a nice layout, and great content all go hand in hand when it comes to effectively presenting your message. You only get one chance to make a first impression so take the time to do it right. You have specific skills and expertise that makes you an expert in coaching rather than in graphic design. Make use of other people's expertise to help you with creating your website and marketing material so you can focus on your areas of strength. They say a picture is worth a thousand words. Don't let your graphics and layout say the wrong words.

Chapter 8: I can't share that! It's confidential!

While it could be unethical to share your confidential client coaching details, there is still a way to make use of some of their results and successes to help grow your coaching business. Ask your clients to create a testimonial of their experience of working with you. Your clients can share the wins and results they got from coaching with you in ways that you cannot. When a client provides you with a testimonial in their own words, it can be a powerful proof element within your overall marketing. Happy clients are very likely to share their success stores in ways that can help bring you more clients. When you have helped them achieve their goals, they are very likely to want to help others achieve the same success by working with you also. Have them use the "before-during-after" format for their testimonial and be sure to have them sign a release so you can use their testimonial in your marketing too.

Chapter 7: Nobody would ever guess...

Your passwords are the only thing between hackers and their free access to using your private information for nefarious purposes. Use strong passwords to make their job as difficult as possible. Be sure to include upper and lower case letters as well as numbers and symbols in your passwords. Longer passwords are harder for hackers to crack. Using a password management tool can greatly simplify not only creating strong passwords, but also remembering them! At a minimum, increase the security of your passwords by substituting some letters with numbers and special characters. Your bank accounts and email aren't the only ones that need strong passwords. Be sure to use them everywhere, and especially on your website for administrator access. Remember: one password – one account. In order to minimize the potential loss, don't reuse passwords - especially when it comes to your email accounts.

Chapter 6: I'll break the internet if I do something wrong!

Website and internet technology may appear to be complex and confusing. However, if you can successfully navigate your way around a word processor, then with only a little more training you can also successfully fix and update your website. WordPress has multiple levels of access built into it so you can easily limit access to the underlying "engine" while still being able to add, update, or change the content of your website. The Editor and

Author roles allow access to pages & posts that can enable you to keep your website content up to date in a "safe" way. Have your webmaster make a backup of your site regularly, and especially before you try your hand at updating your website the first time.

Chapter 5: I'm coaching them; they really don't care what I look like!

You want to be seen on your website by your potential clients. When we are first building a relationship with someone new we want to get to know them. Part of getting to know them is to know what they look like and sound like. Including a welcome video on your website along with a photo of you on your about page can go a long way toward building up the Know-Like-Trust factor with your potential clients. Start by adding a photo at a minimum. While video may seem intimidating to create given the high production value content we see in movies and on TV, YouTube has done a great job of "lowering the bar" for the rest of us. Your potential client is likely to be very pleased to get to know you as a person through a welcome video, even it isn't shot in a professional studio. Simple things like good lighting, clear audio, and a pleasant background can make a big difference in how your video is received, and they are not difficult to arrange. So take the plunge and connect with your potential clients in a way that will make you stand out from the crowd and gain you more coaching clients.

Chapter 4: I found it free on the internet so I can use it, right?

Ignoring copyrights and terms of service can be an expensive mistake to correct. Just because you found it "free" on the internet doesn't necessarily mean you can use it "for free." Through educating yourself with a bare minimum understanding of copyrights by visiting copyright.gov you can avoid some big and potentially costly headaches. Keeping good records and proof of purchase for all content that you acquire will help you avoid a problem if questions ever arise about the content you are using. Be extra careful when working with outsourcers as it's not their business so they may not exercise as much care as you would in this area. Having knowledge and keeping records is your best bet when it comes to staying trouble free.

Chapter 3: CoachFluffyBunny@AOL.com

Part of your professional appearance is a professional email address. You can (and should) have multiple email addresses as part of your business. It is a good idea to make your primary personal business email address YourName@YourBusiness.com. You can auto forward email from most accounts to your primary "convenient" email account. Be sure to stop and think before hitting Send, and ask yourself, "Is this really the account I want to send this email from?" If your business email is being auto forwarded to your "old favorite" email account, you may not really want to reply to your potential coaching client from your CoachFluffyBunny@AOL.com account!

Chapter 2: My ideal clients abhor Social Media, besides I've got a blog!

Social media is here to stay. If you do not have a social media presence you are missing out on a substantial opportunity to grow your influence and promote your coaching business to potential clients you would never be able to touch otherwise. Having a social media plan is a smart thing to do, especially when you take the time to pre-write and gather the images you will use prior to opening the social media site in your browser. Pre-planning along with a little prep work can keep you out of the social media time trap. The social media can be quite rewarding for your business when you use it smartly.

Chapter 1: Look Mommy, I made a website!

Your website is your coaching businesses front door on the internet. You want it to be professional and attractive. You want it to speak to your potential customers in their language. And you want to do it in a way so that they clearly recognize you not only understand their challenges and pain, but are clearly offering something which can specifically help them. Make your site speak to them more clearly by creating your Ideal Customer Avatar, or FRED. Get in side of FRED's head so that you know everything about your Ideal Customer Avatar the same way you know your best friend.

Then speak to them from there in all of your marketing material, including your website. When your ideal client shows up on your "doorstep" and tells you that it was like you were "inside their head" you will know that you've achieved your goal and your coaching practice will be filled with clients you will love to work with for years to come.

Final thoughts

This book has covered a lot of material, some of it more closely related, and other sections are rather diverse. Having an understanding of the material shared here, and more importantly taking action on it, will help you create a coaching business that will thrive where others often fail.

You may think that helping people through coaching is your primary business. In reality your primary focus should be on marketing your business. You can't help anyone if you have no clients to help. You must market your business in order to attract the clients for you to coach. By focusing on marketing your business at least a little bit every day you can be successful. The more effectively you market your business the more easily you will gain clients. Marketing your coaching business is what pays the bills. Effectively marketing your coaching business is how you create an income for yourself beyond just paying the bills. "Marketing" may seem like a dirty word to some. But when you remember, "You can't save the world if you can't pay the rent!" things come into perspective very quickly.

Next steps

The first three mistakes to address (and probably the fastest to fix) are:

- Using strong passwords for all your accounts. Start with your most critical business and personal assets like your bank accounts, email, and website. Then branch out from there.
- Creating and implementing a backup strategy for your computers and website. Investing a little time and money now could save a mountain of hurt later.
- Setting up your professional business email accounts and using them.

Once you have those first three things in place then start working on eliminating the other mistakes. Addressing those first three will give you a solid foundation on which to build a thriving coaching business. Your individual situation will determine which of the other nine mistakes you need to handle next.

Be sure to address all of them. However remember that you will achieve the most leverage in building a thriving business by investing the time and effort in creating your Ideal Client Avatar and ALWAYS speaking to them in everything you do when it comes to marketing your business. You are likely to refine your avatar over time as you come to understand more about how your ideal client expresses their wants, needs, desires, challenges and pains. Your avatar is also likely to need

Conclusion

refinement as you change and learn more about yourself and who your ideal client is..."right now." We all grow and evolve as individuals. Your Ideal Client Avatar will too.

Please make use of the information you've learned in this book to help save the world AND pay the rent! That's my sincere wish for you and your business.

Enjoy!

Brad

Don't Get Left Behind!

Your Personal Invitation from Brad Reed

Because you bought my book, I'd like to invite you to visit my Coaches Marketing Toolbox blog and subscribe for updates and a Bonus Chapter! When you sign up, I will make sure you can get the latest insights into what's working in the world of effectively marketing your coaching business.

If you want to learn what is working when it comes to creating your attractive and effective coaching website, marketing your coaching business, and selling higher ticket coaching packages to your ideal clients, then here's what I'd like to invite you to do.

Go ahead and visit `http://www.CoachesMarketingToolbox.com/book` and sign up for a free account. It takes about 30 seconds and could very well revolutionize the results you get from your marketing and your coaching website.

By signing up you'll be able to get all the latest developments in refining your Ideal Client Avatar so you can speak directly to your ideal client every time, generating interesting and relevant content for your coaching blog that will magnetize your ideal clients to you, and creating an awesome website that you are proud to call your own and show your clients.

So as you are enjoying this book and want to take your coaching website and marketing practices to the next level, head on over to `http://www.CoachesMarketingToolbox.com/book` and get onboard for free. Do it now.

P.S. When you sign up now you will also get access to **Chapter 13**: *Google Is Going To LOVE My Brand New Website!* which is not include in this book. So sign up now and get this exclusive Bonus Chapter!

Recommended Resources

Additional recommended resources may have been added since this book was originally released. Please check here for a complete list of recommended resources and the latest updates:
http://CoachesMarketingToolbox.com/book-resources

Other Books & DVDs By Brad Reed

Fast Migraine Headache Relief With EFT Tapping – Available on Amazon.com
http://amzn.to/1jgbibf

The Secret For Law Of Attraction – Available on Amazon.com
http://amzn.to/1gHVBYs

Additional items may have been published since this book was originally released. Please check here for updates at:
http://CoachesMarketingToolbox.com/published

Your Personal Invitation From Brad Reed:

Visit the Coaches Marketing Toolbox blog and subscribe so you can receive updates and the latest insights into what's working in the world of effectively marketing your coaching business. Visit
http://www.CoachesMarketingToolbox.com/book
to sign up now.

When you sign up now you will also get access to *Chapter 13: Google Is Going To LOVE My Brand*

New Website! which is not include in this book. So sign up now and get this exclusive bonus chapter!

Author Bio

For speaking or consulting inquiries, please contact me through the Coaches Marketing Toolbox Website at: `http://CoachesMarketingToolbox.com/contact`

Chapter 2: Social Media

My With EFT Tapping website blog and Facebook page:
`http://WithEFTtapping.com`

`http://Facebook.com/WithEFTTapping`

Chapter 4: Copyrights

Information on copyrights:
`http://www.copyright.gov/help/faq/faq-general.html`

Recommended royalty free media sites:
`http://CoachesMarketingToolbox.com/media`

Chapter 5: Photos and Video

Current recommendations on creating low cost videos:
`http://CoachesMarketingToolbox.com/video`

Chapter 6: WordPress Roles & Resources

Learn more about how to use the Editor and Author roles in WordPress
`http://CoachesMarketingToolbox.com/wp`

Chapter 7: Passwords

Online password generator tool:
`http://PasswordsGenerator.net`

Information on password managers:
`http://CoachesMarketingToolbox.com/passwords`

Chapter 9: Making A Good First Impression Visually

Information on royalty free website and marketing graphics, audio, and video:
`http://CoachesMarketingToolbox.com/media`

Chapter 10: Email Marketing & Autoresponders

Information on email marketing, autoresponders, and Easy Online Wizards
`http://CoachesMarketingToolbox.com/lists`

Chapter 11: Calls To Action

Information on the Stealth Close Wizard that Creates "Under-The-Radar" Calls To Action
`http://CoachesMarketingToolbox.com/cta`

Chapter 12: Backups

Information on computer and website backup solutions:

http://CoachesMarketingToolbox.com/backup